To Emily
Whose love and spiritual depth
Continue to enrich and fortify me

Acknowledgments

I want to express my appreciation to E. Glenn Hinson, Charles Scalise, Fisher Humphreys, Molly Marshall, and Walter Shurden for their interest in and encouragement in my study of Rauschenbusch. Fred Anderson also has been supportive of my Rauschenbusch study for several years. I want to thank Leslie Andres for her careful and helpful editing of my manuscript. I want to thank Lyndi Wells for typing the earlier version of this manuscript. Her efforts have made mine easier in completing the project. I also want to express my appreciation to my good friend and fellow minister, W. Rand Forder, for a careful proofreading. Finally, I am appreciative of William Smith Morton Library at Union Theological Seminary in Richmond, Virginia, for making available many resources on Rauschenbusch.

Contents

Foreword by Charles J. Scalise — xi
Preface — xiii

Chapter 1: Looking Again at Walter Rauschenbusch — 1
Chapter 2: The Background of the Social Gospel Movement — 13
Chapter 3: A Brief Biography of Walter Rauschenbusch — 25
Chapter 4: The Doctrine of Sin — 43
Chapter 5: The Concept of Personal Salvation — 69
Chapter 6: The Concept of Social Redemption — 91
Chapter 7: Summary and Conclusion — 123

Bibliography — 139
Index — 159

Foreword

Writing a balanced book on Walter Rauschenbusch is no simple task. Rauschenbusch, the principal figure in the American social gospel movement, is a complex prophetic figure. He has been misunderstood and caricatured both by those who think they honor him and those who oppose him as a naïve liberal Protestant academic.

William Tuck has crafted a concise yet well-documented work that uses "the centrality of Rauschenbusch's concept of salvation" (preface, p. xv) to illumine both the evangelical and socialist dimensions of his "both/and" theology. Rauschenbusch's pietism and eleven years of pastoral experience in a poor German Baptist congregation at the edge of New York City's "Hell's Kitchen" grounded him in personal Christian faith and clear-sighted social realism. Though reflecting American pre-World War I optimism, he never succumbed to the dichotomy between personal faith and social justice that split Protestants throughout the twentieth century.

Tuck takes into account the four generations of American academic study and criticism that have sought to analyze Rauschenbusch, but he wears his learning lightly. In lucid prose and judicious primary source quotations (including Rauschenbusch's prayers), Tuck shows the creative gospel-centered balance that united head and heart in Rauschenbusch's life and writings.

This book offers a clearly written introduction to Rauschenbusch for upper-level college students and seminarians, for Baptists and moderate and progressive evangelicals, and for thoughtful readers who want to understand an American prophet who embraced both faith and justice. Rauschenbusch is one of the few Euro-American Christian thinkers of the nineteenth and twentieth centuries whose work continues to illuminate the dilemmas of twenty-first-century Christians and the quest of today's "spiritual but not religious" seekers.

A Revolutionary Gospel should be on the bedside tables and bookshelves, in the backpacks and e-readers of all who seek to understand the not-so-simple gospel in American religious history.

Charles J. Scalise
Professor of Church History
Fuller Theological Seminary

Advance Praise for *A Revolutionary Gospel*

A major addition to Rauschenbusch studies! Impressively researched and cogently argued, *A Revolutionary Gospel* corrects both popular and scholarly misinterpretations of the leading theologian of the Social Gospel and throws new light on the theological underpinnings of that Gospel, notably in Rauschenbusch's understanding of sin and salvation. Written in an engaging style, the book should claim the attention of Rauschenbusch specialists, ethicists, Baptist historians, seminarians, and ordinary saints trying to live a relevant faith in culture not unlike the one Rauschenbusch confronted.

—E. Glenn Hinson
Emeritus Professor of Spirituality and
John Loftis Professor of Church History,
Baptist Theological Seminary at Richmond

Walter Rauschenbusch was the greatest prophet of the Social Gospel, and the Social Gospel is as urgently needed today as it was a century ago when Rauschenbusch was writing about it. In this readable, interesting, and important book, William Powell Tuck, who like Rauschenbusch has served both as a pastor and as a professor, shows that many conventional characterizations of Rauschenbusch's theology simply are not true. This book offers the most even-handed assessment of Rauschenbusch's thought I have read. Rauschenbusch did not minimize personal sin, but he did recognize the power of social sin. He did not deny that God judges sin, but he did affirm that God's judgment is redemptive and restorative. He did not deny the need for a personal salvation, but he did call for society's salvation. He did not claim that Jesus was a social reformer, but he did affirm that Jesus' religious message would lead to social change. He did not deny the future life, but he did affirm the importance of the present life. He was not a utopian optimist who believed that progress is inevitable, but he was a hopeful Christian who believed that the Kingdom of God is coming into the world (as we all pray when we say the Lord's Prayer). He did not identify the Kingdom with democratic America, but he did affirm that God's Reign would be one of justice and peace. And he believed that God intends to work through the church, imperfect though it is, to carry out the divine purposes. If these ideas seem important and true and biblical to you, then I think you will love this book and benefit from it.

—FISHER HUMPHREYS
Professor of Divinity Emeritus,
Samford University, Birmingham, Alabama

Judicious in his use of primary sources, William Tuck brings his thoughtful scholar-practitioner expertise and theological perceptiveness to a fresh study of Walter Rauschenbusch. Addressing an area long debated in the study of this American prophet, Tuck offers a nuanced analysis of Rauschenbusch's articulation of individual and corporate understandings of sin and salvation, especially as they pertain to his vision of the centrality of the Reign of God as present reality. In this lucid delineation of the key theological ingredients of the architect of the theology of the "social gospel," Tuck makes a compelling case for the continuing relevance of his work, especially in our time of growing economic disparity.

—MOLLY T. MARSHALL
President and Professor of Theology and Spiritual Formation
Central Baptist Theological Seminary, Shawnee, Kansas

With this fine, focused book, Tuck advances the relevancy and urgency of Rauschenbusch's work by directly addressing the major criticism against him: that he was "soft" on sin and salvation. As Tuck discovers and conveys, it is precisely in this crucial area of concern where Rauschenbusch offers some of his more inspired contributions to Christian thought.

My hope is that this book points readers not only to Rauschenbusch's work, but leads Christians to more fully know and love Jesus and his redeeming work on earth as in heaven.

—Paul Brandeis Raushenbush
Executive Religion Editor
The Huffington Post

Mentors matter! Our personal teachers matter! Those we read matter! Over fifty years ago, while he was in seminary, Bill Tuck read the works of a fellow Baptist, Walter Rauschenbusch. Rauschenbusch's theology gripped Tuck's mind and soul. Fortunately, Tuck has never escaped that theological grasp. In these pages, Tuck seeks to bring you to Rauschenbusch's understanding of salvation. It is a view of salvation that is both personal and social, a view of salvation that is sorely needed in our world today. My guess is that after you have read Tuck you will want to read Rauschenbusch. Nothing could please Bill Tuck more.

—Walter B. Shurden
Minister at Large
Mercer University

Smyth & Helwys Publishing, Inc.
6316 Peake Road
Macon, Georgia 31210-3960
1-800-747-3016
©2015 by William Powell Tuck
All rights reserved.

Library of Congress Cataloging-in-Publication Data

Tuck, William Powell, 1934-
A revolutionary gospel : salvation in the
theology of Walter Rauschenbusch / by William Powell Tuck.
pages cm
Includes bibliographical references.
ISBN 978-1-57312-804-9 (pbk. : alk. paper)
1. Rauschenbusch, Walter, 1861-1918. 2. Salvation--Christianity. I. Title.
BX6495.R3T83 2015
234.092--dc23

2015006467

Disclaimer of Liability: With respect to statements of opinion or fact available in this work of nonfiction, Smyth & Helwys Publishing Inc. nor any of its employees, makes any warranty, express or implied, or assumes any legal liability or responsibility for the accuracy or completeness of any information disclosed, or represents that its use would not infringe privately-owned rights.

A Revolutionary Gospel

Salvation in the Theology of Walter Rauschenbusch

William Powell Tuck

Also by William Powell Tuck

The Way For All Seasons: Reflections on the Beatitudes for the Twenty-first Century
Facing Grief and Death: Living with Dying
The Struggle for Meaning (editor)
Knowing God: Religious Knowledge in the Theology of John Baillie
Our Baptist Tradition
Ministry: An Ecumenical Challenge (editor)
Getting Past the Pain
A Glorious Vision
The Bible as Our Guide for Spiritual Growth (editor)
Authentic Evangelism
The Lord's Prayer Today
The Way for All Seasons
Through the Eyes of a Child
Christmas Is for the Young . . . Whatever Their Age
Love as a Way of Living
The Compelling Faces of Jesus
The Left Behind Fantasy
The Ten Commandments: Their Meaning Today
Facing Life's Ups and Downs
The Church in Today's World
The Church under the Cross
Modern Shapers of Baptist Thought in America
The Journey to the Undiscovered Country: What's Beyond Death?
A Pastor Preaching: Toward a Theology of the Proclaimed Word
The Pulpit Ministry of the Pastors of River Road Church, Baptist (editor)
The Last Words from the Cross
Overcoming Sermon Block: The Preacher's Workshop
Lord, I Keep Getting a Busy Signal: Reaching for a Better Spiritual Connection

Preface

My first exposure to the writings of Walter Rauschenbusch came in my seminary studies. His application of the gospel to the social order and structures of society intrigued me from my early reading of his writings. I had read Charles Sheldon's book, *In His Steps*, in high school, and it reminded me of the concern of applying the teachings of Jesus to one's everyday experiences of life but in a much wider and more profound context. I learned later that Sheldon's book was one of several novels that addressed the social needs of society in light of the ethical teachings of Jesus. This early introduction to the ethical teachings of Jesus and their application to society, which I had encountered in Shelton, later led to my interest in Rauschenbusch and inspired me to write a Master of Theology thesis on his theology. Throughout my years of ministry, both as a pastor and professor, I have sought to apply Rauschenbusch's teachings to my ministry. Now, some fifty years later, I am still fascinated by his work.

The Kingdom of God was central to Rauschenbusch's theology. He saw it as the first and most essential dogma of the Christian faith and the lost social ideal of Christianity. Jesus' strength was consumed, Rauschenbusch proclaimed, by focusing on making persons aware of God's reign on earth for which he died and for which he promised to return. Rauschenbusch believed that no one could be a Christian in the full sense of discipleship as Jesus taught it until that person made the Kingdom of God the controlling force in his or her life. He did not conceive the Kingdom of God as being concerned with life after death; instead, he viewed it as focused on this world where humanity lives now.[1] The Kingdom, according to Rauschenbusch, was concerned about the redemption of individuals but also focused on the social order in which people lived. Individuals could not be genuinely redeemed without this redemption affecting the social culture around them.

Rauschenbusch believed that Jesus' prayer, "Thy kingdom come; Thy will be done on earth as it is in heaven," was a clear mandate for striving toward that end. We pray here on earth, he said, so "that heaven may be duplicated on earth through the moral and spiritual transformation of humanity, both in its personal units and corporate life."[2] The kingdom became for him the unifying force between religion and all the rest of life—history, science, industry, secular culture, faith, politics, war and peace, the poor, underprivileged, disadvantaged, etc. He affirmed that this kingdom was always both present and future and was always coming but never fully realized in the world. His concept of the Kingdom of God entailed both the religious and ethical concepts of sin and salvation, both the personal and social dimensions of redemption. Salvation to him was seen as sanctification where an individual committed his or her life to Christ and then came under the teachings and discipleship of Christ.

Rauschenbusch projected that this doctrine of the Kingdom could bring about the moral transformation of both the individual and society through the spirit of Christ.[3] "There was a revolutionary consciousness in Jesus; not, of course, in the common use of the word 'revolutionary,' which connects it with violence and bloodshed," Rauschenbusch declared. "But Jesus knew that he had come to kindle a fire on the earth. Much as he loved peace, he knew that the actual result of his work would be not peace but the sword."[4] He believed that Jesus' revolutionary note and reversal, especially in the Beatitudes and teachings like "the last shall be first" and "the greatest among you will be a servant," was clearly evident. He pointed out that Jesus often challenged the ecclesiastical leaders of his day and said their teachings missed the mark and their piety was not real. In *The Righteousness of the Kingdom*, he declared boldly, "Christianity is in its nature revolutionary."[5] And the social gospel he proclaimed was revolutionary in its nature, modeled, he believed, after Jesus' teachings and the Old Testament prophets. He envisioned the present-day Reformation of the social gospel "as a revival of the spirit and aims of Jesus himself."[6] And "the Kingdom ideal," he asserted, "is the test and corrective of the influence of the Church. . . . The Kingdom ideal contains the revolutionary force of Christianity."[7]

To my knowledge, no one has attempted to show clearly the centrality of Rauschenbusch's concept of salvation to his understanding of the Kingdom of God and the rest of his theology. His view of personal and social salvation is essential to an understanding of his teachings. This study has been my effort to address that issue and pay back a debt to Rauschenbusch for the impact his teachings have had on my life and thinking.

Notes

1. Walter Rauschenbusch (hereafter WR), *Christianizing the Social Order* (New York: Macmillan, 1912) 49.

2. WR, *Prayers of the Social Awakening* (Boston: The Pilgrim Press, 1910) 18.

3. WR, *Christianity and the Social Crisis* (New York: Macmillan, 1907) 343ff.

4. Ibid., 185.

5. WR, *The Righteousness of the Kingdom*, ed. Max Stackhouse (Nashville: Abingdon Press, 1968) 70.

6. *Christianizing the Social Order*, 49.

7. WR, *A Theology for the Social Gospel* (New York: Macmillan, 1917) 135.

Chapter 1

Looking Again at Walter Rauschenbusch

An Introduction to Rauschenbusch

More than one hundred and fifty years ago, a man who helped change the course of American Christianity was born. That man was Walter Rauschenbusch, the social gospel's greatest spokesman. Previous to the work of Rauschenbusch, the chief emphasis of Protestant theology was individual salvation and personal righteousness. This emphasis on an individualistic Christianity minimized the relationship of salvation to this world and caused a neglect of social reconstruction. The theology of Rauschenbusch, however, provided an innovation in the conception of salvation and helped many realize the inadequacy of any view of redemption that excluded man and woman's societal involvement. His doctrine called for an expansion in the scope of salvation that would include not only the individual but society as well.

Rauschenbusch prayed for a share in the work of redemption, and that prayer was answered. Though he died in 1918, his message still resounds wherever the social message of Christianity is proclaimed and congregations engage in social actions. Although written forty years ago, the words of James Tull are still true today, I believe: "His [Rauschenbusch's] prophetic stature has been little diminished by the passage of time. He remains a bright ornament in the history of Baptists."[1] The voice of Rauschenbusch has indeed not been silenced. A 1990 edition of *Baptist Theologians* contains a chapter on him.[2] The January 25, 1989, issue of the *Christian Century* had an article about Walter Rauschenbusch and his impact on American religion. Paul Minus published a new biography on Rauschenbusch in 1988.[3] Winthrop Hudson released a volume in 1984 of *Selected Writings* from Rauschenbusch.[4] An article on Rauschenbusch was included in the

Concise Encyclopedia of Preaching, edited by William Willimon and Richard Lischer in 1995.[5] *Christianity and the Social Crisis*, originally published in 1907, was reprinted by Westminster John Knox Press in 1991. In 1997, the same press republished Rauschenbusch's *A Theology of the Social Gospel* in "The Library of Theological Ethics" series, and Donald Shriver denotes Rauschenbusch's continuing importance for ethical and theological thought.[6]

Rauschenbusch's first book was republished by HarperOne on its one hundredth anniversary in 2007 as *Christianity and the Social Crisis in the 21st Century* with a foreword by Rauschenbusch's great-grandson, Paul B. Raushenbush. It carried the tag line, "The classic that woke up the church." Several essays were written in reaction to the book and included in its publication. Phyllis Trible concluded her article with this observation: "One hundred years after the publication of his monumental study, Walter Rauschenbusch the prophet remains the rhetorician for righteousness. In his eloquent appeal to his predecessors, he continues to challenge his successors."[7] In that same book, Stanley Hauerwas concludes his article with these words: "The work he began we must continue. After Rauschenbusch, there is no social gospel that is not 'the social gospel.' We are permanently in his debt."[8] All of Rauschenbusch's books have been reprinted and are available presently; and there are several special editions accessible today of his *Prayers of the Social Awakening* and *Dare We Be Christians*.

The October 9, 1992, edition of *The Whitsitt Journal* was devoted to Rauschenbusch with several articles about his life and contribution along with excerpts from his writings. In 2003, Rauschenbusch was given the "Whitsitt Society Courage Award" posthumously, which was received by his great-grandson, Paul Raushenbush.[9] Another new biography on Rauschenbusch, *The Kingdom Is Always but Coming: A Life of Walter Rauschenbusch*, written by Christopher H. Evans, was published in 2004 and republished in 2009.[10] A chapter on Rauschenbusch by Paul Lewis was included in *Twentieth-Century Shapers of Baptist Social Ethics*, published in 2008.[11] I included a chapter titled "Walter Rauschenbusch: A Prophet for the Social Gospel" in my book *Modern Shapers of Baptist Thought in America* published in 2012.[12] Through the years, many master's and doctor's theses and dissertations have been written about facets of Rauschenbusch's thought and work.[13] PhD dissertations are still being written to examine the thought of Rauschenbusch.[14]

Rauschenbusch was one of the few theologians whose preaching was studied in the collection titled *20 Centuries of Great Preaching*.[15] Although he might not have produced great sermons (by some standards), Rauschenbusch's prophetic message has continued to be heard decades after his death. The social gospel has been called America's unique contribution to the great ongoing stream of Christianity. The primary emphasis of Christianity in the eighteenth and early nineteenth centuries was centered largely on a personal atonement and the necessity of rebirth. This individualistic attitude toward Christianity caused some indifference to the social needs of humanity. Such "orthodoxy" created a strong identification of Christianity with the social order. Rauschenbusch came on the scene and challenged this identification. He believed that one could not interpret the teachings of Jesus' prophetic message about the Kingdom of God without addressing its impact on the social structures of society as well as on the individual. Martin Luther King, Jr., wrote in his essay "Pilgrimage to Nonviolence" that Rauschenbusch had given him much of the theological foundation for his view of nonviolent social change.

Rauschenbusch did a great service for the Christian church by insisting that the gospel deals with the whole man, not only his soul but also his body; not only his spiritual well-being but also his material well-being. It has been my conviction ever since reading Rauschenbusch that any religion that professes to be concerned about the souls of people and is not concerned about the social and economic conditions that scar the soul is spiritually moribund and only waiting for the day to be buried.[16]

Max Stackhouse has challenged the criticism sometimes labeled against Rauschenbusch that his theology "did not treat the central question of Christianity: salvation." Rather than denying the doctrine of salvation, Rauschenbusch's "whole mode of thinking in many ways presupposes 'salvation history . . . ,'" Stackhouse asserts, "and that no definition of salvation is sufficient that does not take account of the social matrix of human existence and a social interpretation of the self."[17] Another writer and former bishop of the Methodist Church and co-president of the World Council of Churches, G. Bromley Oxnam, declared that Rauschenbusch's "teaching, preaching, and writing summoned the religious forces of the nation for the regeneration of society."[18] In her book *Solidarity as Hermeneutic: A Revisionist Reading of the Theology of Walter Rauschenbusch*, Darlene Ann Peitz concludes that Rauschenbusch's work has more than historical significance: "His method and social perspective emerge as distinctly modern. His method of mediation offers an approach to the Christian message which retrieves its radical social gospel for our world today."[19] In a similar way Gary Dorrien declares, "While it is true that much of Rauschenbusch's language, his biblical exegesis, his cultural conservatism, and his optimism are dated, I believe that the core of his work is as relevant as ever."[20] All of these citations—and I could give more—verify the continued importance of Rauschenbusch's theology on our Christian thinking today. I have attempted to lay out in this chapter my approach to examining Rauschenbusch's view of the concept of salvation, which I believe was central to his theological thinking, and I have defined some of Rauschenbusch's terminology to assist the reader in discerning his theological teachings.

An Overview

My purpose in this book is to examine the concept of soteriology (salvation) in the theology of Walter Rauschenbusch in both its personal and corporate aspects. The conceptions of sin and salvation in any theological or religious system are closely correlated. Rauschenbusch's concept of salvation was a theological extension of his doctrine of sin, and this doctrine needs to be understood as a basis for his soteriological views. He conceived of the nature of sin as essentially selfishness and therefore felt that salvation had to be a change that turned man/woman from self to God and to humanity.

Rauschenbusch expressed his view of the solidarity of humanity in his doctrine of original sin in terms of social transmission, and he depicted his concept of satanology as the personification of the supernatural power of evil. These doctrines expressed to Rauschenbusch a solidaristic consciousness of sin. The conception of the racial solidarity of sin resulted in his view of social or corporate redemption. He gave a place in his theology to a discussion of individual sin that resulted in his view of personal salvation, but he believed that an individualistic conception of sin could never be the last word. Even in his view of personal salvation, Rauschenbusch felt that it had to be deeply affected by the solidaristic comprehension furnished by the social gospel. Sin, in his opinion, had to be seen in its individual and corporate aspects and then salvation would be viewed as a unity. Regeneration was for both the individual and society. Rauschenbusch's concept of salvation, therefore, was a natural theological outworking of his doctrine of sin. His social gospel called for an expansion in the scope of sin and salvation, and it resulted in a more thorough concept of salvation.

First, an analysis of Rauschenbusch's doctrine of sin will be made by examining the following concepts: (1) humanity's consciousness of a sinful nature; (2) the nature of sin; (3) the concept of racial solidarity in the doctrine of original sin; and (4) the Kingdom of Evil as it is related to personal sin, collective sin, and satanology. Second, Rauschenbusch's doctrine of salvation will be examined in the following aspects: (1) the concept of personal salvation as expressed in his view of the sacredness of human personality and in the relationship of atonement to the individual; (2) the concept of social redemption as expressed in the relevance of atonement for racial solidarity and its consequences for super-personal entities and the church, which is seen as the social factor in redemption.

Since salvation has always been at the heart of the Christian message, this is a contemporary issue. Rauschenbusch has been considered the social gospel's foremost herald, and therefore his theology has greatly influenced many of the theologians who followed him who were interested in the social aspects of the gospel. No study, to my knowledge, has been made that sought to examine Rauschenbusch's concept of soteriology, and it is felt that this study will provide insight not only into Rauschenbusch's concept of salvation but also into the theological matrix of the theologians influenced by his thought.

The emphasis of some theologians on the "sacramental church" has necessitated a reexamination of Rauschenbusch's view of the church as the social factor in redemption. Also, the present concept of a vast segment of Christendom that salvation is to be conceived only as assent to a set of propositional truths divorced from social action needs to be confronted with Rauschenbusch's view of salvation as an invasion of one's whole life or none of it. These groups, many of whom are fundamentalists, are expounding concepts of an individualistic Christianity that were prevalent in Rauschenbusch's own time. The overemphasis of certain neo-orthodox theologians on the transcendence of God has minimized the relationship of salvation to this world and has caused neglect in social action. Much existentialist philosophy seems close to antinomianism, and thus moral law as it is related to salvation is repudiated. An understanding of Rauschenbusch's concept of soteriology would provide a corrective for many of these present theological weaknesses.

Definitions of Terms Used

Several terms that occur frequently in Rauschenbusch's concept of salvation are briefly defined here. A more complete examination of these terms will be made in the following chapters, so these definitions are not intended to be exhaustive.

- *Soteriology.* This term comes from two Greek words, *soteria* and *logos*, and means "the study of salvation." It is the branch of theology that focuses on salvation for men and women through Jesus Christ. It often deals with the fall (see Gen 3), sin, redemption, atonement, salvation through Jesus' crucifixion, the cross, and grace.
- *Social gospel.* This term was interpreted as the application of the total Christian message of salvation to society as well as to individuals. The social gospel originated as a corrective against an individualistic gospel that negated the relevance of the Christian message of salvation for society. It was not conceived as another gospel but was interpreted as one part of the two phases of the one Christian gospel. The gospel was a unity, but this unity included both the individual and society. (Chapter 2 presents the evolution of this idea in American Protestantism.)
- *Kingdom of God.* The doctrine of the Kingdom of God was to Rauschenbusch the social gospel itself. It was the term used to depict

the ideal social order that would be realized when humanity and societal institutions came under the law or reign of Christ. Rauschenbusch never equated the Kingdom of God with the church, with a future spiritual realm, or with a spiritual quality within people. The Kingdom of God, said Rauschenbusch, is to be objectified on earth, continually growing. The Kingdom of God was conceived as being founded on an inner personal experience with God and was not depicted as being consummated in this world. Nevertheless, the chief significance that Rauschenbusch placed on this doctrine was the possibility of its realization within the social order. The establishing of the Kingdom of God within history was considered in itself as the Christianization of the social order.

- *Racial solidarity.* This term was used to denote how infinitely interwoven was the life of humanity. Man/woman was never depicted by Rauschenbusch as an atomistic individual. Man/woman was seen as an individual ego but never as an isolated ego and was, therefore, always to be seen in his/her relational involvement with humanity. The peculiar form that an individual action took was to be seen as an integral part of the form it took in the social group to which each person belonged. Each person was envisioned as being an integral part of the "organism" of humanity. The action of each person in society deeply affected all, and the action of all deeply affected each person. The concept of solidarity permeated Rauschenbusch's whole doctrine of soteriology. (The usage of this concept is enumerated in chapters 4, 5, and 6.)
- *Super-personal entities.* Super-personal entities were depicted as complex spiritual forces that were beyond the individual. Political parties, business organizations, churches, social groups, and other combinations of individuals were seen as super-personal entities. These forces had the possibility of being in the Kingdom of God when they were under the law of Christ or of being in the Kingdom of Evil when they were under the power of sin. (This concept is discussed more thoroughly in sections of chapters 4 and 6.)
- *Personal salvation.* Personal salvation has been used in the sense that every man and woman has the possibility of experiencing a personal encounter with God. This encounter was depicted as an individual

experience of grace that brought forgiveness of personal sins, but it did not negate man/woman's societal relationship. (Chapter 5 presents a discussion of this concept.)

• *Social redemption.* Social redemption referred to the Christianizing of the social order. It depicted man and woman as being saved from their collective sins and also denoted the bringing of super-personal entities under the law of Christ. Social redemption was the concept that expressed the recognition of collective sins and that viewed sin as being deeply ingrained in society itself. (Chapter 6 is devoted to an examination of the concept of social redemption.)

The Writer's Approach
Overview of Chapters

In the second chapter, an examination of the movement that ushered in the social gospel is delineated. An understanding of the background of the social movement will provide insight into issues that helped create and stimulate the theology of Rauschenbusch. The third chapter offers a brief sketch of Rauschenbusch's life, revealing the personal and social forces that played an integral role in shaping his thought.

The fourth chapter examines Rauschenbusch's doctrine of sin. His concept of salvation is a theological extension of his doctrine of sin, and this doctrine needs to be understood as a basis for his soteriological views. You cannot understand Rauschenbusch's concept of redemption without an understanding of the "sin" from which he believed that man and woman had to be saved. This chapter examines the following aspects of his doctrine of sin: humanity's awareness of sin; the nature of sin; original sin; the Kingdom of Evil; personal sin; collective sin; and satanology.

In the fifth chapter, an examination is made of Rauschenbusch's concept of personal salvation. This chapter reveals that Rauschenbusch did have a substantial view of personal redemption and had not attempted to obscure this doctrine in his emphasis on corporate redemption. The chapter examines the following concepts in the doctrine of personal salvation: sacredness of human personality; the relationship of atonement to the individual; and the influence of the concept of solidarity on individual redemption. The questions raised by the relationship of salvation to mysticism, asceticism, and immortality are also examined.

Rauschenbusch's concept of social redemption is examined in the sixth chapter. This examination includes the following aspects: the social implications of salvation; the atonement and racial solidarity; the redemption of super-personal entities; and the church as the social factor in redemption.

Finally, chapter 7 presents a summary and conclusion of this study.

Sources

The following are among the primary sources used in this study: Walter Rauschenbusch's *A Theology for the Social Gospel*, his last and most mature work; *Christianity and the Social Crisis*; *Christianizing the Social Order*; *Dare We Be Christians*; *Prayers of the Social Awakening*; *The Social Principles of Jesus*; and *Unto Me. The Righteousness of the Kingdom*, a previously unpublished book by Rauschenbusch, was edited by Max L. Stackhouse and published in 1968. Periodicals and other articles by Rauschenbusch have also been consulted. See the bibliography for more details. Vernon P. Bodein's *The Social Gospel of Walter Rauschenbusch and Its Relation to Religious Education* and Dores R. Sharpe's biography, *Walter Rauschenbusch*, have provided many excerpts from some of Rauschenbusch's unpublished manuscripts. Three more recent biographies of Rauschenbusch have been published: *Walter Rauschenbusch: American Reformer* by Paul M. Minus; *The Kingdom Is Always but Coming: A Life of Walter Rauschenbusch* by Christopher H. Evans; and *Rauschenbusch: The Formative Years* by Klaus Juergen Jaehn. *The Rauschenbusch Reader*, compiled by Benson Y. Landis, and Winthrop S. Hudson's edited collection of *Walter Rauschenbusch: Selected Writings* made available some articles that were not obtainable elsewhere for the writer. The following and similar books have been consulted for background and other relevant material, along with many other resources: Christopher H. Evans, editor, *Perspectives on the Social Gospel* and *The Social Gospel Today*; Robert T. Handy, editor, *The Social Gospel in America, 1870–1920*; C. H. Hopkins, *The Rise of the Social Gospel in American Protestantism*;

W. A. Visser't Hooft, *The Background of the Social Gospel in America*; John Dillenberger and Claude Welch, *Protestant Christianity Interpreted Through Its Development*; Ronald C. White, Jr., and C. Howard Hopkins, *The Social Gospel: Religion and Reform in Changing America.*

Notes

1. James Tull, *Shapers of Baptist Thought* (Valley Forge: Judson Press, 1972) 207.

2. *Baptist Theologians*, ed. Timothy George and David S. Dockery (Nashville: Broadman Press, 1990) 366–83.

3. Paul M. Minus, *Walter Rauschenbusch: American Reformer* (New York: Macmillan Co., 1988).

4. Winthrop S. Hudson, ed., *Walter Rauschenbusch: Selected Writings* (New York: Paulist Press, 1984).

5. William McGuire King, "Walter Rauschenbusch," *Concise Encyclopedia of Preaching*, ed. William H. Willimon and Richard Lischer (Louisville: Westminster John Press, 1995) 400–401.

6. Donald W. Shriver, "Introduction to Walter Rauschenbusch," *A Theology for the Social Gospel* (Louisville: Westminster John Knox Press, 1997) xx.

7. Phyllis Trible, "A Rhetorician for Righteousness, Walter Rauschenbusch," *Christianity and the Social Crisis in the 21st Century* (New York: HarperOne, 2007) 79.

8. Stanley Hauerwas, "Repent. The Kingdom Is Here," Rauschenbusch, *Christianity and the Social Crisis*, 176.

9. Paul Raushenbush, "Reflections About My Great-Grandfather, Walter Rauschenbusch," *The Whitsitt Journal*, Fall 2003, 4–6.

10. Christopher H. Evans, *The Kingdom Is Always but Coming: A Life of Walter Rauschenbusch* (Grand Rapids MI: William B. Eerdmans Publishing Co., 2004; repub., Waco TX: Baylor University Press, 2009).

11. Paul Lewis, "Walter Rauschenbusch (1861–1918): Pioneer of Baptist Social Ethics," in *Twentieth-Century Shapers of Baptist Social Ethics*, ed. Larry McSwain & Wm. Loyd Allen (Macon GA: Mercer University Press, 2008) 3–22.

12. William Powell Tuck, *Modern Shapers of Baptist Thought in America* (Richmond VA: Center for Baptist Heritage & Studies, 2012) 32–55.

13. See the unpublished sources in the bibliography.

14. David Bryan True, "Faithful Politics: The Tradition of Martin Luther King, Jr., Reinhold Niebuhr, and Walter Rauschenbusch," PhD diss., Union Theological Seminary and Presbyterian School of Christian Education, Richmond VA, December 2005. See also Heinz D. Rossol, "Walter Rauschenbusch as Preacher: The Development of His Social Thought as Expressed in His Sermons from 1886–1897," PhD diss., Marquette University, 1997.

15. Clyde E. Fant, Jr., and William M. Pinson, Jr., *20 Centuries of Great Preaching* (Waco TX: Word Books Publisher, 1971) 125–72.

16. Martin Luther King, Jr., *Strive Toward Freedom* (New York: Harper & Row, 1958) 91.

17. Max L. Stackhouse, "The Continuing Importance of Walter Rauschenbusch," Walter Rauschenbusch, ed. Max L. Stackhouse, *The Righteousness of the Kingdom* (Nashville: Abingdon Press, 1968) 44.

18. G. Bromley Oxnam, *Personalities in Social Reform* (New York: Abingdon-Cokesbury Press, 1950) 52.

19. Darlene Ann Peitz, *Solidarity as Hermeneutic: A Revisionist Reading of Walter Rauschenbusch* (New York: Peter Lang Publishing, Inc., 1992) 164–65.

20. Gary J. Dorrien, *Reconstructing the Common Good: Theology and the Social Order* (Maryknoll NY: Orbis Books, 1990) 47.

Chapter 2

The Background of the Social Gospel Movement

One cannot understand Rauschenbusch's theology apart from his personality and the age that gave birth to the social gospel. An understanding of the background of the social gospel movement will enrich one's awareness of the significant role Rauschenbusch shared in its development; and a brief sketch of his life in the next chapter will introduce the integral part his personality played in the evolution of his social gospel theology.

In 1917, Rauschenbusch stated that except in backward social or religious communities, the social gospel was no longer a prophetic and occasional note; it had become orthodox.[1] This was probably an overstatement, but the fact that the church by 1917 had enlarged its function to include the social interpretation and application of Christianity was clearly discernible. The social orientation of the church's function had not been a task easy to accomplish. It had taken pioneers and prophets with keen insight into social problems to bring the church to the realization of its social function. Rauschenbusch was heir to the social lineage that preceded him, and in order to understand his social thought, an examination of the movement that engendered the social gospel is necessary.

The social gospel has been called "America's most [sic] unique contribution to the great ongoing stream of Christianity."[2] This indigenous American movement cannot be traced, as a cumulative trend, beyond the "gilded age" of the 1880s.[3] The Christian philosophy of the eighteenth and early nineteenth centuries had been centered largely on individualism and placed great emphasis on the substitutionary atonement and the necessity of rebirth. This individualistic attitude toward Christianity caused indifference to the social needs of humanity and placed the burden of responsibility on a comparatively small group of religious leaders.[4]

American Protestant interest in social Christianity found its real beginning in the post Civil War years when it responded to the challenge of modern industrialism. Before this challenge, however, four aspects of thought in the mid-nineteenth century influenced the development of the social movement. (1) The first emphasis of orthodox Christianity was on the salvation of the individual while social consequences were left to take care of themselves. Life was viewed in the medieval pietistic concept as a period of testing with heaven as a reward for individual virtue or suffering. Like the vivid portrayal of "Christian" in John Bunyan's *Pilgrim's Progress*, the Christian was pictured as being on a pilgrimage from this world to the heavenly world. (2) Under the influence of the new scientific thought and the new industrial situation, an enlightened orthodoxy contributed a progressive attitude that paved the way for the social gospel in people's concept of the humanity of Jesus and in their view of the possibility of actualizing the Kingdom of God in this world. The views of progressive orthodoxy that the Kingdom was social and terrestrial as well as heavenly and spiritual helped formulate the "new theology" of the 1880s and later developed into the "modernism" of the twentieth century. (3) Conventional evangelicalism envisioned that the necessary revolutionary change in society was to come by divine initiative. Revivalism had constructed a wall of separation between the present world and the heavenly world, and the realization of the Kingdom of God in this world was seen as the needed resolution to terminate this dualistic concept. (4) The Unitarians were ahead of their contemporaries in social concerns and pioneered in emphasizing the ethical character of the Kingdom and the social message of Jesus.[5]

The social gospel movement developed as a reaction against the uncritical identification of Christianity with the existing social order. In *Protestant Christianity Interpreted through Its Development*, John Dillenberger and Claude Welch relate three aspects of Protestantism to society that effectuated this reaction. The first factor they enumerate is a change in the attitude of Protestantism toward the world. Although conservative Christianity in the mid-nineteenth century had placed the emphasis on "this world" as being mainly a place of preparation, Protestantism as a whole seemed to have changed in its attitude toward the world. This change, Dillenberger and Welch say, resulted in a more positive attitude toward the political, economical, and cultural achievements of the world. The roots of this new attitude were seen as partially coming from the influence of the "humanism" of the Renaissance, the "this-worldly" emphasis of Calvinism, and the development of science and the growth of commerce.[6]

The second aspect of this changing attitude may be seen in the development of the idea of the "calling" or vocation that symbolized the role of the Christian in the "secular" world. The reformers had rejected the superiority of "religious" vocations over lay or secular vocations and stated that the distinction was only a matter of function. Calvin's view that every aspect of a person's life can be the means of exhibiting the glory of God opened the way for a new attitude toward commerce and finance. This concept of vocation in the reformers and especially Calvin indicated that the commercial enterprise was no longer to be viewed as inherently evil but could be employed as the fulfillment of one's religious duty to God.[7] R. H. Tawney has suggested that there was a close correlation between Calvinism and the development of capitalism.

In all countries alike, in Holland, in America, in Scotland (in Geneva itself), the social theory of Calvinism went through the same process of development. It had begun by being the very soul of authoritarian regimentation. It ended by being the vehicle of an almost Utilitarian individualism. While social reformers in the sixteenth century could praise Calvin for his economic rigor, their successors in Restoration England, if of one persuasion, denounced him as the parent of economic license, and if of another, they applauded Calvinist communities for their commercial enterprise and their freedom from antiquated prejudices on the subject of economic morality.[8]

Soon, however, the Calvinistic ideal faded almost to obscurity and was replaced by a distinction between the specifically "religious" and secular interest that emasculated religion and made it merely a private matter, leaving the realm of economic engagement to its own laws of self-interest. The theory of the harmony of interest gave a semblance of morality to the free-enterprise economics and placed divine sanction on them. Adam Smith's *Wealth of Nations*, 1776, gave the classical expression of this theory of free-enterprise economics. This new concept was either an abandonment of the societal ideal of Calvinism or the synthesis of Christianity and civilization, which identified the Christian societal goals with free enterprise, democracy, and patriotism. The *laissez-faire* concept of economy was seen as being grounded in the laws of God and nature, and Protestantism placed its stamp of approval on the social, political, and economic status quo.[9] Bill Leonard notes that the social gospel came about in part as a response to the "so-called Gospel of Wealth" that was fostered by certain clergy and laity including Andrew Carnegie, the industrialist and philanthropist who espoused that God had chosen certain people to have large amounts of money to benefit society.[10]

Henry Ward Beecher, the eloquent orator of Plymouth Church, Brooklyn, is a vivid example of the defenders of the status quo in America. Although his large salary and many royalties received from his books and articles enabled him to drive fine horses and carry a handful of uncut gems in his pocket, Beecher condemned the railroad employees in 1877 for not being willing to bear their conditions of poverty in a more noble manner.

> It is said that a dollar a day is not enough for a wife and five or six children. No, not if the man smokes or drinks beer. It is not enough if they are to live as he would be glad to have them live. It is not enough to enable them to live as perhaps they would have a right to live in prosperous times. But is not a dollar a day enough to buy bread with? Water costs nothing; and a man who cannot live on bread is not fit to live. What is the use of a civilization that simply makes men incompetent to live under the conditions which exist?[11]

Philips Brooks, another outstanding Protestant clergyman of this period, seemingly unaware of the social tension of his age, wrote in

1887 that "excessive poverty, actual suffering for the necessities of life, terrible as it is, is comparatively rare."[12]

The third factor in the relation of Protestantism to society was seen in the priority given to the life to come, which resulted in the relative unimportance associated with the inequalities and hardships of this life. It would be unjust to say that Protestantism placed no restraints on the economic and social area. But the Christian responsibility was seen as a matter of individual stewardship or as an attempt to correct specific abuses in the "working" of the social system. Social measures of the gospel were seen in the area of prison reform, the abolition of the slave trade, improvement of factory conditions, and the fight against child labor. Although these reforms were significant, they did not attempt to change the system itself but only specific abuses within the system. These reforms were to make life more tolerable, but religion was concerned mainly with the priority of the life to come.[13]

The uncritical identification of Christianity with the existing social order engendered forces both within and outside the institutional church that fostered the development of the social movement. Marxist socialism made the most vociferous external attack on the position that the church assumed toward society. In the *Communist Manifesto* and *Das Kapital*, Marx had stated that history was determined by economic forces and that religion was only "a product of economic forces" and "an instrument" that the capitalist class used to sustain power and exploit workers. Religion was viewed as "the opiate of the people."

The appearance of Marxism was of great importance in the mid-nineteenth century for two reasons. First, Marxist socialism pronounced judgment on the social exploitation and injustice that resulted from the Industrial Revolution. Christianity had failed to do this. Second, the Marxist view of a perfect society was similar to the Christian concept of the Kingdom of God on earth, except in Marxism the religious foundation was displaced by economic terminology.[14]

The external attack of Marxism was met by forces within the church that had already been awakened to the failure of the church in effectuating the social implication of its message. The Christian socialists of England, especially F. D. Maurice and Charles Kingsley, were calling for social reform the same year that the *Communist Manifesto* was published. They tried to improve working conditions through religious regeneration, to form producers' cooperatives and trade unions, and to promote popular education. Their influence was slight in their own day, but they helped greatly in the later development of the social message in England.[15]

The birth of the social gospel in America was confronted by four types of nineteenth-century problems. These problematic situations were the unrestricted competition of classical economics, the conflict between labor and capital, business ethics, and the problems of urban life.[16] The social gospel pioneers called for the church to open its eyes to the social problems encompassing it and to be a protagonist in effectuating a solution for these problems. Washington Gladden, often called "the father of the social gospel," wrote concerning these problems and said,

> Now that slavery is out of the way, the questions that concern our free laborers are coming forward; and no intelligent man needs to be admonished of their urgency. They are not only questions of economy, they are in a large sense moral questions; nay, they touch the very marrow of that religion of good-will of which Christ was the founder. It is plain that the pulpit must have something to say about them.[17]

Rauschenbusch paid tribute in *Christianizing the Social Order* to three men he considered as pioneers in Christian social thought in America: Washington Gladden, Josiah Strong, and Richard T. Ely.[18] Gladden's influential social works were *Workingmen and Their Employers*, 1876; *Applied Christianity*, 1887; and *Tools and the Man*, 1893. Men and women were compelled to examine the social problems when they read Josiah Strong's *Our Country*, 1886; *The New Era*, 1893; and *The Next Great Awakening*, 1902. An economist, Richard T. Ely, in his book *Social Aspects of Christianity*, challenged the economic system with his understanding of the Christian message.

Edward Bellamy, George D. Herron, Francis G. Peabody, Shailer Mathews, and many others could be listed to show the growth of social concern that had gradually infiltrated the Protestant church.[19]

The name "social gospel" was coined and popularized by Ralph Albertson in a newspaper titled *The Social Gospel* that was published for more than three years and read by liberal thinkers across America. The paper's name gradually became accepted as the name for social Christianity.[20] The acceptance of this name for the social movement in Christianity was clearly seen in Shailer Mathews's work *The Social Gospel* published in 1910, and Rauschenbusch's last book *A Theology for the Social Gospel* written in 1917.

The social gospel was proclaimed by organizations such as the Brotherhood of the Kingdom, Christian Social Union, and the Church Association for the Advancement of the Interests of Labor.[21] Such popular hymns as Frank Mason North's "Where Cross the Crowded Ways of Life," Gladden's "O Master, Let Me Walk With Thee," and Ernest Shurtleff's "Lead On, O King Eternal" were mediums of expressing the social message.[22]

A unique form of expressing the social message, however, was seen in the social gospel novel. Gladden's *The Christian League of Connecticut*, R. E. Porter's *The Union League Club*, and Edward Everett Hale's *How They Lived in Hampton* are examples of this type of literature.[23] Probably the most successful of these novels was *In His Steps: What Would Jesus Do?* by Charles Monroe Sheldon. This novel has been ranked with *Uncle Tom's Cabin* and *Ten Nights in a Bar Room* as a classical American tract. *In His Steps* was estimated in 1933 to have sold more than 23,000,000 copies throughout the English-speaking world and to have been translated into twenty-one foreign languages.[24] Although these novels were often individualistic in their conception of Christianity and utopian in their solutions, they served to awaken social religion in millions of laypeople who might never have been reached otherwise.

To understand the rise of the social gospel in American Protestantism, one needs to be aware that it was an indigenous American movement influenced by the age in which it was born. Probably the greatest factor in its engenderment was the intensity of the social problems themselves.[25] But the influence of Puritan theology, the contribution of the enlightenment and revivalism,[26] and the influence of the physical sciences, evolution,[27] and liberal theology,[28] especially biblical criticism, assisted in the development of the social movement in America. The official recognition of the social gospel was seen in the establishment of the Federal Council of the Churches of Christ in America in 1908.[29] This organization was brought into being from the influence of social action and was to be a medium of expressing the social concern of the churches in America. The Federal Council of Churches has been called "the lengthened shadow of Walter Rauschenbusch" and is considered one of the mediums through which "he lives and speaks" today.[30]

Christopher Evans has challenged the church of the twenty-first century to discover the relevance of the message of some of the original social gospel proponents to find the meaning for our lives today, not to embrace all aspects of their theology but to arrive at fresh insights for our own day.[31] Our task, he asserts, is to find adequate expressions from their teachings that are timeless in nature and relevant to us. He believes that the social gospel is one tradition that "calls upon Christians to wrestle with how the ramifications of a distinctive tradition can enable us who care about the church's future to engage the complex social realities of our era."[32] In papers that were presented at the Inaugural Social Gospel Conference at Colgate Rochester Divinity School in 1998 (collected in a book, *Perspectives on the Social Gospel*, by Christopher Evans), some of the presenters raised the imperative that future studies of the social gospel not only examine the specific historical contours of the past but also note how "the theologies spawned by the Social Gospel tradition support contemporary concerns for social action."[33] Max Stackhouse and others involved in this study believe that the social gospel is not dead. Stackhouse affirms that it is alive and well in the preoccupations of many thinkers and preachers, and has generated a number of public initiatives that have continued by entering, altering, and intermixing with other movements and developments in various social and religious spectrums of twentieth-century thought.[34]

Peter Gomes, former Plummer Professor of Christian Morals and Pusey Minister in the Memorial Church at Harvard University, reminds us that the gospel was social to begin with because it was too important to be left alone in the church as it was propounded by Jesus to be applied to society. He saw that a Christian society needed to have a zeal for social reform as it sought to enable a passive Christian society to apply the good news to society's most pressing needs.[35] Gomes does not believe that the gospel of Jesus was bifurcated into a spiritual gospel and a social gospel. It is all one, he observes. It is the whole gospel for the whole person. He even quotes from Richard Land, who asserted that "The idea that there are two Gospels, a social one and a spiritual one, was hatched in the pits of hell. There's only one Gospel, and it's the whole Gospel for whole people." Gomes is not sure if Land has limited his understanding of the only one gospel to terms of individual and private relations with God. If so, he says he disagrees with him. He saw a change in society as a part of Jesus' original gospel as well as a personal individual change.[36] At face value, Land's quote is on target for the social gospel advocates. Gomes and others have seen the gospel of Jesus as a continuing challenge to "reform" society as well as a call for personal redemption in our twenty-first century.

Notes

1. Walter Rauschenbusch, *A Theology for the Social Gospel* (New York: The Macmillan Company, 1917) 2.

2. Charles Howard Hopkins, *The Rise of the Social Gospel in American Protestantism, 1865–1915* (New Haven: Yale University Press, 1940) 3.

3. John Bennett, "The Social Interpretation of Christianity," *The Church Through Half a Century*, ed. Samuel McCrea Cavert and Henry P. Van Dusen (New York: Charles Scribner's Sons, 1936) 113.

4. Shailer Mathews, "Social Gospel," *A Dictionary of Religion and Ethics*, ed. Shailer Mathews and Gerald B. Smith (Chicago: The Macmillan Company, 1922) 416. See also Mathews, "The Development of Social Christianity," *Religious Thought in the Last Quarter-Century*, ed. Gerald B. Smith (Chicago: University of Chicago Press, 1927) 229.

5. Hopkins, *Rise of the Social Gospel*, 14–22.

6. John Dillenberger and Claude Welch, *Protestant Christianity Interpreted through Its Development* (New York: Charles Scribner's Sons, 1954) 232–33.

7. Ibid., 234.

8. R. H. Tawney, *Religion and the Rise of Capitalism* (London: John Murray, 1948) 227.

9. Dillenberger and Welch, *Protestant Christianity*, 236.

10. Bill J. Leonard, *Baptists in America* (New York: Columbia University Press, 2005) 31.

11. Henry Ward Beecher, *Christian Unions*, 1 August 1877, p. 93, quoted by Henry F. May, *Protestant Churches and Industrial America* (New York: Harper and Brothers, 1949) 94.

12. Quoted by Francis P. Weisenburger, *Ordeal of Faith* (New York: Philosophical Library, 1959) 129.

13. Dillenberger and Welch, *Protestant Christianity*, 237–38.

14. Ibid., 239–41.

15. Ibid., 242.

16. Hopkins, *Rise of the Social Gospel*, 24.

17. Ibid. Hopkins quoting Washington Gladden's *Workingmen and Their Employers*, 3.

18. WR, *Christianizing the Social Order* (New York: The Macmillan Company, 1912) 9.

19. For the most scholarly and complete account of the development of the social gospel movement in American Protestantism, see Hopkins, *The Rise of the Social Gospel in American Protestantism*, and Ronald C. White, Jr., and C. Howard Hopkins, *The Social Gospel: Religion and Reform in Changing America* (Philadelphia: Temple University Press, 1976). See also Robert T. Handy, "Social Gospel," 593–94 in *The Westminster Dictionary of Christian Ethics*, ed. James F. Childress and John Macquarrie (Philadelphia: The Westminster Press, 1986); Christopher H. Evans, ed., *Perspectives on the Social Gospel* (Lewiston NY: The Edwin Mellen Press, 1990), and Christopher H. Evans, ed., *The Social Gospel Today* (Louisville: Westminster John Knox Press, 2001).

20. Hopkins, *Rise of the Social Gospel*, 196.

21. Ibid., 319.

22. Dillenberger and Welch, *Protestant Christianity*, 246.

23. Hopkins, *Rise of the Social Gospel*, 140–41.

24. Ibid., 140–43.

25. May, *Protestant Churches and Industrial America*, 91–160. May's thesis is that the Protestant Churches during the "gilded age" were in a period of complacency and had to be awakened by the intensity of the social problems that could no longer be ignored. See Harold Underwood Faulkner, *The Quest for Social Justice, 1898–1914*, vol. 11 of A History of American Life, ed. Arthur M. Schlesinger and Dixon R. Fox, 12 vols. (New York: The Macmillan Company, 1931) 204–28.

26. For a discussion of the influence of Puritan theology, the enlightenment, and revivalism on American Protestant social thought, see W. A. Visser't Hooft, *The Background of the Social Gospel in America* (Haarlem: H. D. Tjeenk Willink and Xoon, 1928) 66–144. For an excellent treatment of revivalism and the social movement, see Timothy L. Smith, *Revivalism and Social Reform* (New York: Abingdon Press, 1957).

27. For the importance of science as an influential factor in American social thought, see Walter Marshall Horton "Science and Theology," *The Church Through Half a Century*, ed. Cavert and Van Dusen, 93–101; Weisenburger, *Ordeal of Faith*, 61–79; Hopkins, *Rise of the Social Gospel*, 123–34; and Visser't Hooft, *Background of the Social Gospel*, 145–68.

28. For the role of liberal theology in American social thought, see John Wright Buckham, *Progressive Religious Thought in America* (Boston: Houghton Mifflin Company, 1919); Hopkins, *Rise of the Social Gospel*, 55–66; Weisenburger, *Ordeal of Faith*, 80–116, 180–87; Henry P. Van Dusen, "The Liberal Movement in Theology," *The Church Through Half a Century*, ed. Cavert and Van Dusen, 67–84; Kenneth Cauthen, *The Impact of American Religious Liberalism* (New York: Harper & Row, 1962); L. Harold DeWolf, *The Case for Theology in Liberal Perspective* (Philadelphia: The Westminster Press, 1959); Henry P. Van Dusen, *The Vindication of Liberal Theology: A Tract for the Times* (New York: Charles Scribner's Sons, 1963).

29. Hopkins, *Rise of the Social Gospel*, 302. See also Raymond H. Bailey, *Destiny & Disappointment* (Wilmington NC: Consortium Books, 1977) 15.

30. Dores Robinson Sharpe, *Walter Rauschenbusch* (New York: The Macmillan Company, 1942) 406.

31. Evans, *The Social Gospel Today*, xiv–1.

32. Ibid., 10.

33. Evans, *Perspectives on the Social Gospel*, xviii.

34. Ibid., xi.

35. Peter J. Gomes, *The Scandalous Gospel of Jesus* (New York: HarperOne, 2007) 165.

36. Ibid., 176–77, quoting Richard Land, *Real Homeland Security: The America God Will Bless* (Nashville: Broadman & Holman, 2004) 177.

Chapter 3

A Brief Biography of Walter Rauschenbusch[1]

Walter Rauschenbusch has been called the "American Savonarola"[2] and is considered "the social gospel's greatest prophet."[3] The significance of the life of this Baptist historian has been acclaimed by Henry P. Van Dusen as "the greatest single personal influence on the life and thought of the American church in the last fifty years."[4] He put him in a class with Jonathan Edwards and Horace Bushnell "as one of the three most influential men in the thought of the American church."[5] Max Stackhouse linked Rauschenbusch with the lineage of Edwards and Bushell but added Ralph Waldo Emerson and suggested that his inheritance from these people could be traced in their own ways to Herman Melville, Abraham Lincoln, and William James. Stackhouse also felt that it was important "to recover, at least in part, that prophetic tradition as exemplified in Walter Rauschenbusch, for we are in a day when 'cheap prophecy' is as much a danger to the American churches as 'cheap grace' was to the Germany of Dietrich Bonhoeffer a generation ago."[6] Ambrose Vernan has described him as "perhaps the most creative spirit in the American theological world";[7] while Reinhold Niebuhr has estimated that Rauschenbusch was "not only the real founder of social Christianity in this country but also its most brilliant and generally satisfying exponent to the present day."[8] Martin Luther King, Jr., said Rauschenbusch contributed to American Protestantism "a sense of social responsibility that it should never lose."[9] Stephen Branchlow saw Rauschenbusch as a unique combination of evangelical commitment and social consciousness.[10]

"Rauschenbusch played his prophetic social role," Paul Minus concludes, "as part of a more vast historical movement—a reformation that brought far-reaching change to the churches, renewing their theology and worship, challenging their divisions, expanding their geographical base, and refocusing their mission to the world."[11] "Probably more than any other single individual of his time," according to William Ramsay, "he [Rauschenbusch] changed the nature of mainline American Protestantism."[12] William King felt that Rauschenbusch's social gospel in its stress on "revolutionary Christianity" foreshadowed contemporary liberation theology.[13] In an analogous way, Harvey Cox declared that "long before the term 'liberation theology' was minted, Rauschenbusch was teaching and preaching a similar theme."[14] Christopher Evans argued that although Rauschenbusch believed that he was helping Christianity rediscover the true meaning of the ancient gospel message of Jesus, he was "the propagator of a new genre of Christianity that changed the way Christianity would be interpreted in America."[15] Paul Lewis affirms that Rauschenbusch "serves to model a Christian ethic that is both firmly rooted in the Christian tradition and does not require Christians to abdicate their mission in and to the world." Continuing, he states that Rauschenbusch "contributes to the wider world of Christian Social Ethics in a fruitful model for theological/ethical method."[16] Kenneth Cauthen declares, "If William Adams Brown was liberalism's most eminent teacher, and Harry Emerson Fosdick its foremost preacher, then Walter Rauschenbusch was liberalism's greatest prophet."[17]

In his graduation thesis from Rochester Baptist Seminary in May 1886 titled "The Ethics of Thinking," also used later as a commencement address, Rauschenbusch said,

> Service now involves poverty, reproach, and that awful loneliness—the loneliness of thinking the thought alone among your brethren. Others shrink from speaking out the new truth because they dread the consequences, not for themselves, but for others. For what truth has ever been born into this world without agony? The new cannot live except by destroying the old. And as that crashes to the ground, it bears with it all the time-honored institutions resting upon it.[18]

Rauschenbusch did not shrink from proclaiming his concept of truth for fear of the consequences; instead, he resolved to live literally by the teachings and spirit of Jesus so that he might "share in the work of redemption."[19] The influence of Rauschenbusch's writings reveals the important contribution that his message made in the ongoing stream of Christian social thought. But one cannot understand this message or its success completely without knowing something about the man who proclaimed it.

Walter Rauschenbusch was born October 4, 1861, in Rochester, New York, to German parents who had migrated to the United States seven years earlier. His father, August Rauschenbusch, was the sixth in a direct line of clergymen, but had become a Baptist, breaking with the family's Lutheran tradition. For thirty years his father taught in the German Department at Rochester Theological Seminary.[20] Rauschenbusch wrote that his father "was very strict with his children, but he was also a caring and loving father."[21] One of his earliest memories of his father was when he was about three years old, and his father was playing "*fangen*" (a German game of catch or tag) with his three children. He remembers running down the street until they captured him by his arms, legs, and coattails.[22] But Rauschenbusch describes his father as autocratic and influenced by the old school in Germany. The relationship between his father and mother was often bitter and hostile. He wrote to his father from Germany once, interceding for his mother, and said, "You cannot imagine how the quarrels at home have oppressed us children."[23] His father also had long absences from home. Except for the intervention of his mother, the young Rauschenbusch would likely have run away from home to escape his father's capricious authority. Nevertheless Rauschenbusch was still influenced by his father in many ways, especially in his quest for learning.[24]

Born in this scholarly tradition, Rauschenbusch studied in the United States and in Germany, mastering Latin, Greek, French, German, and Hebrew.[25] He studied at the Evangelische Gymnasium zu Gutersloh, a private secondary school, in Westphalia, Germany. He was called "the energetic American" and graduated with the top rank in his class as the student body's *Primus Omnium*.[26] In 1884 he graduated from the University of Rochester and in 1886 from the English Department of the Rochester Theological Seminary.[27] At the age of seventeen he had a vital personal religious experience that changed his whole perspective of life. He never sought to minimize the necessity of one's personal relationship to God, and he described his own conversion experience in the following manner:

> And then, physically, came the time of awakening for me . . . and what I said to myself was: "I want to become a man; I want to be respected; and if I go on like this I cannot have the respect of men." This was my way of saying: "I am out in a far country and I want to get home to my country and I do not want to tend hogs any longer," and so, I came to my Father, and I began to pray for help and got it; and I got my own religious experience.
> . . . Such as it was, it was of everlasting value to me. It turned me permanently and I thank God with all my heart for it. It was a tender mysterious experience. It influenced my soul down to its depths. Yet, there was a great deal in it that was not really true.[28]

Later, with his deeper educational training, he would reevaluate that experience and recognize his emotional input as well as his spiritual upheaval, but he would never lose the glow or power of the vital personal experience he felt that day. Rauschenbusch had wanted to go as a missionary to India, but his appointment by the American Baptist Foreign Mission Society was blocked because of his liberal views of the Old Testament that one of his professors at the seminary, Howard Osgood, had noted.[29] According to Christopher Evans, however, Rauschenbusch was given another invitation to reapply for the missionary post as president of the Telugu Baptist Seminary at Ramapatnam in southern India in April 1887.[20] By this time, though, Rauschenbusch had turned in his twenty-fifth year to accept a call to the second German Baptist Church in New York City with only one hundred and twenty-five members and at a salary of nine hundred dollars a year, three hundred dollars of which had to go for rent. For eleven years he worked among the poverty-stricken congregation situated on the edge of "Hell's Kitchen," one of the city's notorious slums.[31] The neatly dressed clergyman often appeared before the New

York City council and made a plea for a playground with sand piles for children in his neighborhood, for help for "fallen" girls who became unwed mothers, for employers to pay living wages for their workers, for better sanitation facilities in the tenements, for inspections to enforce safety provisions to give assistance to ill, aged, handicapped, and unemployed, and for help with other social problems.[32] A butcher who was a member of Rauschenbusch's church said of his pastor, "We have found in Pastor Rauschenbusch more that is Christlike than in any human being we have ever met."[33]

These eleven years left a profound impression on the mind of Rauschenbusch. Here he saw that the "conventional picture" of his religious fathers failed to meet the complete needs of the endless procession of men "out of work, out of clothes, out of shoes and out of hope."[34] These experiences with the "heartbeat" of society gave birth to his awareness of the necessity for a social application of the gospel. John Macquarrie declared that Rauschenbusch's concern for the working class led him to believe that the evils of industrial society move us to socialism.[35] "A socialist solution," Rauschenbusch wrote, "should be hailed with joy by every patriot and Christian."[36] "Religion is the only power which can make socialism succeed if it is established," he declared. "It cannot work in an irreligious country."[37] Douglas Ottati also notes that Rauschenbusch identified himself as a "practical socialist."[38] Robert Handy states that Rauschenbusch accepted the label of a Christian socialist, but his socialism was non-political and non-doctrinaire, and he never became a party member because he did not trust the materialistic philosophy.[39]

In 1912 an intimate friend of Rauschenbusch, F. W. C. Meyer, wrote concerning the factors that led to Rauschenbusch's concept of social Christianity and said, "Henry George and Bellamy and Mazzini and Karl Marx and Tolstoy influenced him some, but above all the crying need of the comfortless multitude and the senseless inadequacy of competitive strife, the apparent possibility of cooperative service and jubilant remedy of the message of the Kingdom took hold of his susceptible soul."[40] His great concern for the endless procession of needy men and women who "wore down our threshold and wore away our hearts"[41] formulated in Rauschenbusch a drive to find an answer to the immense social problems they confronted. In his effort to serve his church in "Hell's Kitchen," he arose too soon from his sickbed and lost his hearing as a result.[42] But the cry of the needy had reached his ears, and he was never to forget the suffering cry of humanity. His deafness often caused him to be shy and sensitive and at times resulted in severe loneliness, but he never complained nor let it spoil his spirit. A Rochester professor, Clarence A. Barbour, in speaking of Rauschenbusch's deprivation, said that he "bore it with a smile; did not allow it to interfere with that gracious and sparkling humor of his which was so marked a characteristic of his thinking and his word."[43]

Rauschenbusch stated that he owed his first awakening to the world of social problems to the influence of Henry George in 1886.[44] This awakening drove Rauschenbusch back to a renewed study of the New Testament, and he became convinced that his social concern and principles were verified by the teachings and ideals of Jesus.[45] Prior to 1886 he had been reading sermons and books on personal problems by D. L. Moody, Edward Judson, Alexander MacLaren, J. Hudson Taylor, Henry Drummond, Robert Hasting, and John A. Broadus; but now his attention was directed to the study of social issues. The economic thought of Rauschenbusch was influenced by the leading economic authorities of his day: Paine Gilman, Graham Taylor, E. A. Ross, Jacob Riis, and many others. *The Captive City of God* by an English nonconformist minister, Richard Heath, also had a profound influence on Rauschenbusch's social thinking.[46]

His social philosophy was also influenced by John Ruskin, F. D. Maurice, Leo Tolstoy, Karl Marx, Henry George, Giuseppe Mazzini, Edward Bellamy, and J. S. Mill and by a wide reading among other scholars.[47] In theology Rauschenbusch acknowledged his debt to Friedrich Schleiermacher and Albrecht Ritschl, and he was also affected by Josiah Royce's philosophy of loyalty and Adolf Harnack's concept of history.[48] When Rauschenbusch was called by his fellow Baptists a "social gospeler," this depiction implied that he "was unorthodox, if not downright heretical."[49]

In 1889–1891, Elizabeth Post, J. E. Raymond, Leighton Williams, and Rauschenbusch attempted to publish a paper devoted to the interest of the working people of New York City. The paper, *For the Right*, attacked the forces of greed, monopoly, and maldistribution, as well as the conditions of labor from the viewpoint of Christian socialism.[50] *The New York Times* commented that *For the Right* was "radical, yet Christian, and says boldly what in their opinion every pulpit in New York ought to be saying."[51] In *For the Right* Rauschenbusch had written on economic and industrial issues, on politics, on the separation of church and state, on religion, and on the Kingdom of God, and had sought to arouse the working men to a consideration of the whole social question.[52] The voice of the paper soon ceased, but while it lasted it served as a powerful medium for Rauschenbusch to formulate and express his social ideas.

In December 1892, in the city of Philadelphia, Rauschenbusch, Leighton Williams, Nathaniel Schmidt, Samuel Zane Batten, and about seven others formed an organization known as the "Brotherhood of the Kingdom." The group was formed to bring about the realization of the ethical and spiritual principles of Jesus in their individual and social aspects. The members pledged to exemplify obedience to the ethics of Jesus in their personal lives and to propagate the thoughts of Jesus to the best of their ability. They sought to stress the social aims of Christianity and to keep themselves in contact with the common people in hopes of infusing the religious spirit into the efforts for social amelioration in the world.[53] The purpose of the Brotherhood of the Kingdom was set forth by Rauschenbusch in the following statement:

> We desire to see the Kingdom of God once more the great object of Christian preaching; the inspiration of Christian hymnology; the foundation of systematic theology, the enduring motive of evangelistic and missionary work, the religious inspiration; the object to which a Christian man surrenders his life, and in that surrender save it to eternal life; the common object in which all religious bodies find their unity; the great synthesis in which the regeneration of the spirit, the enlightenment of the intellect, the development of the body, the reform of political life, the sanctification of industrial life, and all that concerns the redemption of humanity shall be embraced.[54]

To this task the group called the Brotherhood of the Kingdom dedicated their lives, and for more than twenty years they met every summer for a week discussing the things that later came to be called the social gospel. Here within their group, religion was freed from dogma and sociology was unshackled from materialism, and both were fused into a unity purified of their dross and made relevant for the deeper needs of humanity.[55] The discussions, addresses, and prepared papers that were exchanged in the Brotherhood gave Rauschenbusch an opportunity to develop what became his central theological motif: the Kingdom of God.

Often overlooked in the life of a great man is his wife. But in examining the life of Rauschenbusch one finds that his wife cannot be left unmentioned. He married Pauline Rother, a Milwaukee school teacher, in 1893, and she not only created a warm home atmosphere but also assisted her husband as counselor and constant companion in his expanding ministry. She was able to communicate with considerable finesse the gist of a conversation to her husband. This was of great service to Rauschenbusch, especially when he needed to make a quick reply at meetings when questions were directed to him.[56]

Rauschenbusch was a devoted husband and a tender and loving father toward his five children. In a 1917 letter to his son, Hilmar, he wrote, "There is no love available to you which is so unvarying and always trustworthy as the love of your mother and father. . . . You must help us make the transition from parenthood to friendship."[57] His home served as an oasis where he could be renewed in spirit and encouraged by the tenderness of love. A few months after they were married, Pauline wrote to her husband, "what a heaven this earth would be if everyone had a husband like mine."[58] He once described his home as a "well-spring of life and a refuge from the storm."[59] Unfortunately as his children began to grow into young adulthood, they were reluctant to receive Baptist baptism, and tension grew in other family differences. Rauschenbusch did not want to be as stern as his father had been, but his children's attitude and rebellion troubled him and he was not certain how to respond to them effectively.[60]

He experienced what most normal parents do in the maturing of their children.

In seminary, Rauschenbusch had told a classmate that he wanted to be a pastor, and "if I do become anything but a pastor, you may believe that I have sunk to a lower ideal or that there was a very unmistakable call to a duty in that direction."[61] That "unmistakable call" eventually came from the seminary from which he had graduated and where his father had taught for many years. In 1897, Rauschenbusch began his teaching career at the Rochester Theological Seminary, first in the German Department and five years later in the English Department as professor of Church history.[62] For twenty-one years as a professor, he had a pronounced influence upon his students not only as a scholar and as a social reformer but also through the possession of a dynamic personality and the admirable manner in which he handled his deafness. Henry B. Robins, a former student and a fellow teacher with Rauschenbusch at Rochester, said that "within the field he [Rauschenbusch] chose to develop he moved as a master."[63] Rauschenbusch was a stimulating professor, and his carefully prepared and interestingly delivered lectures always had a profound effect on the students. "He breathed into history the breath of life, and history became a living thing."[64] In a course he offered at the seminary on the "Devil," he was amused when he was told that students would ask one another, "Are you going to the Devil with Ruschie?"[65] In this elective course, Rauschenbusch traced the history of the personalized concepts of the principle of evil, which was an illustration of the use of history in the development of his thought.[66]

The most far-reaching influence exerted by Rauschenbusch came through his writings. He had written for a number of scholarly journals in German and English and had translated many articles from German into English, including "Letters to Thomas Muntzer by Conrad Grebel and Friends," which was published originally in *The American Journal of Theology* and used as the source for a revision later published in volume 25 of The Library of Christian Classics.[67] Rauschenbusch wrote four books in German: *The Life of Jesus*, 1895; *Biography of Augustus Rauschenbusch*, 1901; *Civil Government in the United States*, 1902; the section on the "United States" in Gustav

Krüger's *Handbook der Kirchengeschichte*, 1909. He also edited several German hymnals with translations of selected hymns from English into German. His first book in English, *Christianity and the Social Crisis*, published in 1907, established him at once as the recognized leader of the social gospel movement. In this book he discussed the religious development of the prophets of Israel, the life and teachings of Jesus, the primitive church, and the development of the church up to the present time in order to determine the original and fundamental purpose of Christianity. The essential purpose he envisioned was the Kingdom of God. The "present crisis" was then depicted and the stake of the church in the present social movement enumerated. This book had the largest sale of all his books, more than fifty thousand copies, and was published in 1937 and republished in 2007 by HarperOne.[68]

His second book in English, *Prayers of the Social Awakening*, published in 1910, reveals the unusual quality and spiritual depth of the author's soul. Personal prayer was the source of his vitality, and he expressed in another article the significance he had found in prayer.

> Prayer is the most distinctively religious act. Morality is the outcome of religion; it is the test of religion; but it is not religion itself. A man may be a just and loving man, but if he does not pray, he lacks something in the sight of God and he lacks something in the depths of his own consciousness that he might have had and which would give a stronger sweep to his soul, a rare fragrance to his love, a braver poise to his walk.[69]

Rauschenbusch considered his book of prayers as a pioneering project, and in it he attempted to make prayer more than merely an individualistic affair. He sought to socialize prayer. This book should not be considered one of the minor works of Rauschenbusch because it was one of his most influential and one of his most quoted. Josiah Strong said that "it will be recognized as the Thomas á Kempis of Social Christianity.[70]

Using his Merrick Lectures presented at Ohio Wesleyan University and the Earl Lectures delivered at the Pacific Theological

Seminary as a nucleus, Rauschenbusch wrote *Christianizing the Social Order* in 1912. This book was the most systematic and complete exposition of Rauschenbusch's position on social problems and the relationship of the Christian message to them. He soon penned three smaller books: *Unto Me*, 1912; *Dare We Be Christian?* 1914; and *The Social Principles of Jesus*, 1916. *The Social Principles of Jesus* was written for the College Voluntary Study Course series and was an attempt to formulate the fundamental convictions of Jesus about the social and ethical relationship and duties of men.[71] Rauschenbusch also translated many hymns into German. In one German hymnal that had 272 translations, he had translated 127 of them in simple and picturesque words.[72]

A Theology for the Social Gospel was Rauschenbusch's last and probably his greatest work and was delivered as the Nathaniel W. Taylor Lectures at Yale Divinity School in 1917. Because of his fear of the social gospel losing its religious character, he sought to give a systematic theology large enough to match the social gospel and vital enough to support it. He gave attention to the doctrines of sin and salvation with their social implications and in this light touched on revelation, inspiration, baptism, the Lord's Supper, eschatology, the atonement, and the concept of God and the Holy Spirit. As in all of his books, he placed the Kingdom of God at the center of his argument.

Again, Rauschenbusch's central theological concept was the Kingdom of God. He believed this concept was the heart of the teaching of Jesus. To him, the Kingdom of God was not merely a concept or an ideal but a historical force. He gave his best thought to this ideal, and he based his social gospel on it. "This doctrine is itself the social gospel. Without it, the idea of redeeming the social order will be but an annex to the orthodox conception of the scheme of salvation."[73]

Rauschenbusch did not conceive of the Kingdom of God as simply an external objective force that could be built by man/woman; he envisioned it as being founded on an inner personal experience of faith that is internally engaged upon and that has to be externally expressed if it is to survive or be meaningful. To him, the Kingdom of God was the social gospel, and through this truth he sought to direct the thoughts of men and women toward an active Christianity that would move and pulsate throughout the whole of human society.

Although Rauschenbusch had received wide acclaim for his writings from many quarters, he still had critics like William B. Riley, a Baptist cofounder of the Christian Fundamentalist Association, and others who denounced him as a modernizing liberal.[74] His unwillingness to be a strong critic of Germany in their atrocities in Belgium and France, which ushered in World War I, led many to question his patriotism. His summer cottage in Ontario was vandalized several times. Many of his friends and followers distanced themselves from him, and some invitations to speak were withdrawn. He was grieved not only by the war but also by the fact that some felt he had a "disloyal preference" for Germany when in reality he had made clear his preference for America.[75] Rauschenbusch had prayed that God would not let him be stranded in a lonesome and useless old age, and on July 25, 1918, at the age of fifty-seven with the shadow of World War I across his path, he died from cancer. The war had presented a challenge to the social gospel, and he felt that the social gospel needed to be lifted into the international arena in order to combat war, which he considered the most sinful thing that existed—a major part of the Kingdom of Evil. When illness had overtaken him and death drew near, he said, "Since 1914 the world is full of hate, and I cannot expect to be happy again in my lifetime."[76] A private memorial service was held two days after his death at the Rauschenbusch home. In October a memorial service was held at the Rochester Seminary, and an issue of the school journal for the first time was devoted to a deceased faculty member with words of praise for his life and ministry.[77]

One of the most vivid summary statements ever written on Rauschenbusch was delivered by Conrad Henry Moehlmann, professor at Rochester Theological Seminary, at the Memorial Service for Rauschenbusch on November 18, 1918.

> How universal he was: Ideal husband and father, citizen of Rochester, of Boston, and of the Kingdom of God, minister at a weak city church, without his equal in the forum movement, shepherd of the poor and insignificant and oppressed of every race,

friend unfailing in humor, in wisdom and suggestion, co-founder of the Brotherhood of the Kingdom, secretary so many years of the Baptist Congress, "bridge-builder" for thousands without hope, translator of hymns that have circled the globe, contributor to the daily press and monthly magazine, editor of religious periodicals, author of many published books and called home with several others under contemplation, prophet capable of the invective of Amos but manifesting the tenderness of Hosea, poet so modest that even the circle of his friends remained unaware of his genius, man of prayer whose devotional spirit will continue to be present at family reunions, in corridor and ward of hospital, in sweat-shop and prison, in custom house and on the battlefield, lover of babies and children, grand international soul who championed democracy, the brotherhood of man, the co-operative commonwealth, genuine seeker after God and at all times and everywhere a child of God.[78]

The good that Rauschenbusch accomplished was not "interred with his bones" but lived after him and has exerted a lasting influence not eroded by time. In January 1961, Rauschenbusch's *A Theology for the Social Gospel* was republished in a paperback edition by Abingdon Press, and it was republished in 1997 by Westminster John Knox Press, signifying the continuous interest in his far-reaching thought. Many people have acknowledged their indebtedness to him, including Harry Emerson Fosdick,[79] Martin Luther King, Jr.,[80] Kagawa, John Haynes Holmes, Francis J. McConnell, and countless others.[81] Ten years after Rauschenbusch's death, Justin Wroe Nixon wrote in *The Colgate-Rochester Divinity School Bulletin* that Rauschenbusch was a teacher of extraordinary learning and insight who was "the foremost interpreter in his time of modern social Christianity, poet, mystic, saint, prophet of new reformation in religion, he was the greatest human being some of us have ever known."[82]

The lasting influence that Rauschenbusch exerted on individuals and society has been best described by his biographer in the following statement:

> Today the Rauschenbusch influence, thought somewhat more vague and indefinable than during his more active years, is

nonetheless real and pervasive. Rauschenbusch threw the boulder of social responsibility into the deep but stagnant waters of Christian consciousness; the waves are still spreading in ever-widening circles. They will continue to do so until they reach the farthest shores of man's social responsibility. Then will the kingdom have come in beauty, and glory, and majesty, in the earth.[83]

Notes

1. I have read the three biographies on Rauschenbusch by Dores R. Sharpe, *Walter Rauschenbusch* (1942), Paul M. Minus, *Walter Rauschenbusch: American Reformer* (1988), and Christopher H. Evans, *The Kingdom Is Always but Coming: A Life of Walter Rauschenbusch* (2004). Unless some material has added to or changed my knowledge of Rauschenbusch's life, I have made my first reference to Sharpe's original biography. Some material in this chapter was adapted from my chapter on Rauschenbusch in *Modern Shapers of Baptist Thought in America* (Richmond VA: Center for Baptist Heritage & Studies, 2012) 32ff.

2. *The Publisher's Weekly Book Review* quoted by *The Rochester Theological Seminary Record*, November 1918, p. 46.

3. John Dillenberger and Claude Welch, *Protestant Christianity Interpreted through Its Development* (New York: Charles Scribner's Sons, 1954) 247.

4. Cited in Dores Robinson Sharpe, *Walter Rauschenbusch* (New York: The Macmillan Company, 1942) 247.

5. Cited in George L. Hunt, ed., *Ten Makers of Modern Protestant Thought* (New York: Association Press, 1958) 31.

6. Max L. Stackhouse, "The Continuing Importance of Walter Rauschenbusch," in Walter Rauschenbusch, *The Righteousness of the Kingdom*, ed. Max L. Stackhouse (Nashville: Abingdon Press, 1968) 14.

7. Ambrose White Vernon, "Later Theology," *The Cambridge History of American Literature*, vol. 3 (New York: Macmillan Company, 1936) 215.

8. Reinhold Niebuhr, *An Interpretation of Christian Ethics* (New York: Harper and Brothers, 1935) preface.

9. Martin Luther King, Jr., "Pilgrimage to Nonviolence," *The Christian Century* 77 (1960): 439.

10. In Timothy George and David S. Dockery, eds., *Baptist Theologians* (Nashville: Broadman Press, 1990) 378–79.

11. Paul M. Minus, *Walter Rauschenbusch: American Reformer* (New York: Macmillan Co., 1988) 176.

12. William M. Ramsay, *Four Modern Prophets: Walter Rauschenbusch, Martin Luther King, Jr., Gustavo Gutierrez, Rosemary Radford Ruether* (Atlanta: John Knox Press, 1986) 10.

13. William McGuire King, "Walter Rauschenbusch," in *Concise Encyclopedia of Preaching*, ed. William H. Willimon and Richard Lischer (Louisville: Westminster John Knox Press, 1995) 401.

14. Harvey Cox, back cover of Christopher H. Evans, *The Kingdom Is Always but Coming: A Life of Walter Rauschenbusch* (Grand Rapids MI: William B. Eerdmans Publishing Co., 2004).

15. Evans, *The Kingdom Is Always but Coming*, xxx.

16. Paul Lewis, "Walter Rauschenbusch (1861–1918): Pioneer of Baptist Social Ethics," *Twentieth-Century Shapers of Baptist Social Ethics*, ed. Larry L. McSwain and Wm. Loyd Allen (Macon GA: Mercer University Press, 2008) 17.

17. Kenneth Cauthen, *The Impact of American Religious Liberalism* (New York: Harper & Row Publishers, 1962) 107.

18. In Sharpe, *Walter Rauschenbusch*, 57.

19. Walter Rauschenbusch, *Prayers of the Social Awakening* (New York: Pilgrim Press, 1917) 117.

20. Benson Y. Landis (comp.), *A. Rauschenbusch Reader* (New York: Harper and Brothers, 1957) xiv.

21. August and Walter Rauschenbusch, *Life and Ministry of August Rauschenbusch* (Sioux Falls SD: Sissons Printing, Inc., 2008) 170.

22. Ibid., 170–71.

23. In Gary Dorrien, *The Making of American Liberal Theology: Idealism, Realism, & Modernity 1900–1950* (Louisville: Westminster John Knox Press, 2003) 75.

24. Susan Curtis, *A Consuming Faith: The Social Gospel and Modern Culture* (Baltimore: John Hopkins University Press, 1991) 104–108.

25. Sharpe, *Walter Rauschenbusch*, 44.

26. Minus, *American Reformer*, 19–21.

27. Sharpe, *Walter Rauschenbusch*, 58.

28. Ibid., 43.

29. Ibid., 58.

30. Evans, *The Kingdom Is Always but Coming*, 43–44.

31. Sharpe, *Walter Rauschenbusch*, 59–60.

32. O. K. Armstrong and Marjorie M. Armstrong, *The Indomitable Baptists: A Narrative of Their Role in Shaping American History* (Garden City NY: Doubleday & Company, Inc., 1967) 192–96.

33. D. R. Sharpe, *The Social Gospel of Rauschenbusch* (New Haven CT: Yale University Press, 1944) 79, quoted in Armstrong & Armstrong, *The Indomitable Baptists*, 196.

34. In Ray S. Baker, *The Social Unrest* (New York: 1910) 268, quoted by Hopkins, Charles Howard Hopkins, *The Rise of the Social Gospel in American Protestantism, 1865–1915* (New Haven: Yale University Press, 1940) 216.

35. John Macquarrie, *Twentieth Century Religious Thought: The Frontiers of Philosophy and Theology, 1900–1960* (New York: Harper & Row Publishers, 1963) 164.

36. WR, *Christianity and the Social Crisis* (New York: Macmillan Company, 1907) 408.

37. In Armstrong & Armstrong, *The Indomitable Baptists*, 203.

38. Douglas F. Ottati, "Social Gospel," 448, in *A New Handbook of Christian Theology*, ed. Donald W. Musser and Joseph L. Price (Nashville: Abingdon Press, 1992).

39. Robert T. Handy, ed., *The Social Gospel in America, 1870–1920* (New York: Oxford University Press, 1966) 261.

40. Sharpe, *Walter Rauschenbusch*, 216–17. Hopkins quoting F. W. C. Meyer, "Walter Rauschenbusch, Professor and Prophet," *The Standard*, 3 February 1912, p. 662.

41. Benjamin E. Mays (comp.), *A Gospel for the Social Awakening* (New York: Association Press, 1950) 14–15.

42. Sharpe, *Walter Rauschenbusch*, 66.

43. *The Rochester Theological Seminary Record*, 6.

44. WR, *Christianizing the Social Order* (New York: Macmillan Company, 1912) 394.

45. Sharpe, *Walter Rauschenbusch*, 64.

46. Ibid., 64–66.

47. Ibid., 197.

48. Hopkins, *The Rise of the Social Gospel*, 220.

49. Armstrong & Armstrong, *The Indomitable Baptists*, 193.

50. Sharpe, *Walter Rauschenbusch*, 64. The only known available file of *For the Right* is in the Yale Divinity School Library. In 1968, Abingdon Press published this material in an edition of *For the Right*, edited by Max Stackhouse.

51. Ibid., 88. Sharpe quoting *The New York Times*, November 1890.

52. Vernon Parker Bodein, *The Social Gospel of Walter Rauschenbusch and Its Relation to Religious Education* (New Haven: Yale University Press, 1944) 10.

53. Ibid., 17–19.

54. Ibid., 18–19. Bodein quoting from Rauschenbusch, "The Brotherhood of the Kingdom," *The National Baptist* (c. 1893).

55. Sharpe, *Walter Rauschenbusch*, 139.

56. Ibid., 71–72.

57. Quoted in Curtis, *A Consuming Faith*, 112.

58. Evans, *The Kingdom Is Always but Coming*, 113.

59. Sharpe, *Walter Rauschenbusch*, 76.

60. Minus, *American Reformer*, 190ff. See also Evans, *The Kingdom Is Always but Coming*, 236ff.

61. Sharpe, *Social Gospel of Rauschenbusch*, 54, quoted in Armstrong & Armstrong, *The Indomitable Baptists*, 194.

62. Sharpe, *Walter Rauschenbusch*, 141–42.

63. *The Rochester Theological Seminary Record*, 33.

64. Sharpe, *Walter Rauschenbusch*, 143.

65. Armstrong & Armstrong, The Indomitable Baptists, 199.

66. Robert G. Tolbert, *The Baptist Ministry Then and Now* (Philadelphia: Judson Press, 1953) 118–19.

67. WR, *The American Journal of Theology* 9 (1905): 91–99. Cited with revised translation in "Letters to Thomas Muntzer by Conrad Grebel and Friends," in George Huntston Williams, ed., *Spiritual and Anabaptist Writers*, vol. 25 of The Library of Christian Classics, ed. John Baillie et al. (Philadelphia: Westminster Press, 1957) 73–85.

68. Sharpe, *Walter Rauschenbusch*, 158. The book sold 55,000 copies in three years and was the best selling book after the Bible then. The book was republished in 1937, 1961 (Abingdon Press), 1997 (Westminster/John Knox), and 2007 (HarperOne). The total number of copies sold to date is unknown, but it would be in the thousands.

69. Ibid., 272.

70. Ibid., 282.

71. WR, *The Social Principles of Jesus* (New York: Association Press, 1917) introduction.

72. Armstrong & Armstrong, *The Indomitable Baptists*, 322.

73. WR, *A Theology for the Social Gospel*, 131.

74. Dorrien, *The Making of American Liberal Theology*, 124.

75. Ibid., 118.

76. Sharpe, *Walter Rauschenbusch*, 356.

77. Minus, *American Reformer*, 194.

78. *The Rochester Theological Seminary Record*, 17–18.

79. Harry Emerson Fosdick, *The Living of These Days* (New York: Harper and Brothers, 1956) 107.

80. Martin Luther King, Jr., "Pilgrimage to Non-violence," *The Christian Century* 77 (13 April 1960): 440.

81. Sharpe, *Walter Rauschenbusch*, 417.

82. Justin Wroe Nixon, "Biographical Walter Rauschenbusch," Stanley Irving Stuber, comp. and ed., *The Christian Reader: Inspirational and Devotional Classics* (New York: Association Press, 1955) 473.

83. Sharpe, *Walter Rauschenbusch*, 418–19.

Chapter 4

The Doctrine of Sin

Mary Frances Thelen has made the accusation that "teachers of the philosophy of religion and systematic theology in the major liberal seminaries during the first third of the twentieth century have little in their writings on the subject of sin."[1] H. Richard Niebuhr spoke of the inadequacy of the optimism of the social gospel preachers and their view of sin in these words: "A God without wrath brought men without sin into a kingdom without judgment through the ministrations of a Christ without a cross."[2] Although John Bennett had noted that critics of the social gospel had criticized this movement beyond all fairness, he still was one of the more influential critics when he avowed that the movement had underestimated the degree to which sin is inexorable in all social and personal contexts, which meant that it did not take into account the tragic dimension in history.[3] An examination of the works of Rauschenbusch shows that this charge cannot be justified when directed against him. Although a teacher of church history and making no claims to be a doctrinal theologian, Rauschenbusch was an innovator in giving a theology for the social gospel. In his Taylor Lectures, he enumerated that the sections of theology that would be profoundly affected by the social gospel and give an adequate expression to it were the doctrines of sin and redemption.[4] Gary Dorrien noted that in these lectures Rauschenbusch devoted six consecutive chapters to a discussion of sin.[5]

The conceptions of sin and salvation in any theological or religious system are closely related. Rauschenbusch's concept of salvation was a theological extension of his doctrine of sin, and this doctrine needs to be understood as a basis for his soteriological views. Abstract speculation was not the parent to Rauschenbusch's idea of sin; instead, his concrete relationship with humanity, especially his eleven years in the West Side of New York City, was the cause of its engenderment.

His social gospel called for a reexamination and expansion in the scope of sin and therefore resulted in a more thorough concept of salvation. This chapter, then, will examine Rauschenbusch's doctrine of sin under the following divisions: humanity's awareness of sin; the nature of sin; original sin; and the Kingdom of Evil as reflected by personal sin, collective sin, and satanology.

Human Awareness of Sin

Rauschenbusch was fully aware that one of the causes for distrusting the social gospel was that it often failed to give an adequate place to the power and guilt of sin. The responsibility for sin was frequently unloaded on the environment and the individual was not awakened to his or her own responsibility. In acknowledging the partial truth of this accusation, Rauschenbusch cautioned that the old theology, however, had its equivalents for environment. It placed the responsibility on original sin, on the devil, and on the decrees of God.[6]

But Rauschenbusch realized that humanity by its very nature was involved in tragedy and therefore stated that "any religious tendency or school of theology must be tested by the question whether it does justice to the religious consciousness of sin."[7] The basis of all doctrines of sin, he affirmed, was found in the Christian consciousness of sin that deepens as our moral insight matures and becomes religious.

Man and woman's awareness of his or her involvement in sin was expressed by Rauschenbusch in the following manner:

> To lack the consciousness of sin is a symptom of moral immaturity or of an effort to keep the shutters down and the light out.... In childhood and youth we have imperious instincts and desires to drive us, and little knowledge to guide and control us. We commit acts of sensuality, cruelty, or dishonor, which nothing can wipe from our memory. A child is drawn into harmful habits which lay the foundations for later failing, and which may trip the man again when his powers begin to fail in later life.... The weakness of the stubbornness of our will and the tempting situations of life combine to weave the tragic web of sin and failure of which all make experience before we are through with our years.[8]

Man/Woman has found that sin is so powerful a force that it has invaded one's whole being and all that one touches. Rauschenbusch held up as a caricature of Christianity the chief marks of a Christian that were stated by an eminent minister in New York as being attending church, reading the Bible, and contributing to the church's financial support. Likewise, he held up in disdain as poor insight into the reality of sin the notion that the four sins from which a Christian had to abstain were drinking, dancing, card playing, and going to the movies.[9] Traditional theology, he stated, had "strained at gnats and swallowed camels" by putting the emphasis on minor sins and overlooking the major wrongs of humanity and society.

Rauschenbusch analyzed with acute insight the failure of traditionalism's consciousness of sin in his story of the Mennonite farmer in Toronto. In Toronto, if the milk was found too dirty by the health inspector, the cans were emptied and marked with large red labels. On finding his cans labeled one day, a Mennonite farmer used profane language and was brought before his church and excluded. "But mark well," Rauschenbusch enumerated, "not for introducing cow-dung into the intestines of babies, but for expressing his belief in the damnation of the wicked in a non-theological way."[10] The failure of this church, Rauschenbusch believed, was in not seeing that the farmer's use of profanity in anger was a private matter that he could settle alone with God and that the major sin lay in his use of the defiled milk supply that would put the life and health of the young children in jeopardy. This was the major sin for which the farmer needed to repent.[11]

The old theology was viewed by Rauschenbusch as side-stepping the seriousness of sin as it related to societal morality, and he called men and women to a new baptism of repentance.

> Our duty to the Kingdom of God is on a higher level than all other duties. To aid it is the supreme joy. To have failed it by our weakness, to have hampered it by our ignorance, to have resisted its prophets, to have contradicted its truths, to have denied it in time of danger, to have betrayed it for thirty pieces of silver,—this is the most poignant consciousness of sin.[12]

The Nature of Sin

In attempting to define the nature of sin, Rauschenbusch found the task as elastic and complicated as life itself. Humanity by its human nature was equipped with powerful appetites, and in one's experiment with life these appetites often go astray. The degree to which a person's intelligence and will enter determines when sin becomes guilt. In a person's self-love, he or she desires to satisfy these limitless cravings that, if expressed without restraint, result in crippling one's higher self and injuring society.[13]

Rauschenbusch has discerned sin as essentially selfishness. This definition of sin was to him more basically Christian than the dualistic conception of the Greek Fathers, who viewed sin as essentially sensuousness and thought the chief consequence of the fall was the reign of death rather than the reign of selfishness. As the character of sin matures, the element of selfishness first emerges, and then in the higher forms of sin the selfish ego and common good of humanity are in conflict. Expressed in religious terms, it becomes a conflict between self and God.[14] "The three forms of sin,—sensuousness, selfishness, and godlessness,—are ascending and expanding states, in which we sin against our higher self, against the good of men, and against the universal good."[15]

When Rauschenbusch depicted a person's rebellion against God, he repudiated the concept that it was a solitary duel of the will between a man or woman and God. He viewed this concept as a product of the monarchical institutions that demanded a person's first duty to the royal will while one's relationship to the rest of the realm was another matter.[16] "Sin is not a private transaction between the sinner and God," he wrote. "Humanity always crowds the audience-room when God holds court. We must democratize the conception of God; then the definition of sin will become more realistic."[17]

Rauschenbusch's concept of sin as essentially selfishness and not as a solitary rebellion against God has drawn criticism and misunderstanding. Waldo Beach has written that his concept had a realism that was not characteristic of the later social gospel exponents. Yet he continues by stating, "But even Rauschenbusch shared the dominant liberal conviction in viewing sin in primary 'horizontal' terms, as selfishness in defiance of neighbor-needs, rather than primarily as the rebellion of the will against the sovereignty of God."[18]

Robert T. Handy makes a similar accusation against Rauschenbusch: "In defining sin as essentially selfishness he [Rauschenbusch] did less than justice to the classic Christian understanding of sin as pride."[19] However, whether one can surmise that the only Christian understanding of sin is pride remains open to debate. E. A. Burtt has stated that there are two prominent views of sin in the Bible. One view is that the essence of sin is rebellious disobedience against God, and the other view locates the root of sin in man and woman's lustful cravings of the flesh that war against the aspirations of the spirit.[20]

Paul Tillich has stated that *hubris*, the Greek word usually translated as pride, should not be translated as "pride," for pride is a moral quality and its opposite is humility.[21] He enumerates his position in the following argument.

> *Hubris* is not one form of sin beside others. It is sin in its total form, namely, the other side of unbelief or man's turning away from the divine center to which he belongs. It is turning toward one's self as the center of one's self and one's world.... And it is in the totality of his personal being that man makes himself the center of his world. This is his *hubris*; this is what has been called "spiritual sin."[22]

Reinhold Niebuhr, who has defined sin as primarily pride, states, "again it cannot be claimed that Christian thought is absolutely consistent in regarding pride as the basic sin."[23] He continues his thought on sin by explaining that "the definition of sin as pride is consistently maintained in the strain of theology generally known as Augustinian."[24] In order to show the validity of this latter statement, he gives quotations from Augustine, Pascal, Luther, Thomas Aquinas, and Calvin. But it appears to the writer that Rauschenbusch would be in basic agreement with these statements. Niebuhr gave Pascal's definition of sin as being "essentially unjust in that it makes self the centre of everything and it is troublesome to others in that it seeks to make them subservient."[25] This definition sounds similar to Rauschenbusch's statement that human sinfulness stands out in true proportion when one seeks to establish a private kingdom of self-service and stands ready to thwart and defeat the progress of mankind in order to establish it.[26]

In his analysis of sin, Niebuhr has distinguished four types of pride: pride of power, pride of knowledge, pride of virtue, and spiritual pride that rises out of the third type.[27] Although Niebuhr has defined sin as primarily pride, he is soon using selfishness and pride interchangeably.[28] Often, it would appear, this struggle over a formal definition of sin is reduced to an absurd battle of jargon. Hans Hofmann has also pointed out that sin to Niebuhr is never something that takes place merely between God and individuals but has different consequences and manifestations in the relationship of man and woman to society.[29] This aspect of Niebuhr's concept of sin is enumerated in the following statement in his Gifford Lectures:

> The Bible defines sin in both religious and moral terms. The religious dimension of sin is man's rebellion against God, his effort to usurp the place of God. The moral and social dimension of sin is injustice. The ego which falsely makes itself the center of all existence in its pride and will-to-power inevitably subordinates other life to its will and thus does injustice to other life.[30]

Although Rauschenbusch and Niebuhr have given different formal definitions of sin, Richard Dickerson's statement that "Rauschenbusch and Niebuhr are brothers under the theological skin" seems basically correct.[31] Niebuhr and Rauschenbusch have different formal conceptions of sin, but Niebuhr's understanding of sin as pride finds it counterpart in his predecessor's understanding of sin as selfishness—a term more suited to demonstrating the effects of sin in social and individual life.[32]

George Hammar's accusation that sin in Rauschenbusch's theology is not primarily sin against God but is identified only with an unsocial attitude is similar to the criticism of Beach and Handy.[33] But this is a misunderstanding of Rauschenbusch's thought. Rauschenbusch made no claims of being a systematic theologian, and one does not find a systematized theology among his writings. His Taylor

Lectures were an attempt to give the social gospel a theology, but they were not a systematic treatment of his theology. He did not dwell at length on topics that he realized were already acceptable and orthodox but stated that "the social gospel is the old message of salvation, but enlarged and intensified."[34] Although Rauschenbusch does not give a systematic doctrine of sin, he nowhere implied that sin was merely an unsocial attitude. When we undertook to define the nature of sin, we accepted the old definition, that sin is selfishness and rebellion against God, but we insisted on putting humanity into the picture.[35]

Rauschenbusch accepted sin as rebellion against God but not in the sense of a lone person standing on a deserted island shaking his or her fist at God while repudiating the divine will and asserting his or her own. A person rarely sins against God alone. H. Shelton Smith has remarked that Rauschenbusch viewed man and woman's sin as including interpersonal involvements but that "Rauschenbusch had no intention of obscuring the radical nature of sin as supremely a revolt against God."[36] The involvement of man or woman with society in his or her sins had been left largely unrealized by the individualistic theology. Rauschenbusch saw that individuals rarely sin against God alone, and therefore his concept of sin became an expansion rather than a distortion of this rebellion. He wrote, "We love and serve God when we love and serve our fellows, whom he loves and in whom he lives. We rebel against God and repudiate his will when we set our profit and ambition above the welfare of our fellows and above the kingdom of God which binds them together."[37]

God as the spiritual representative of humanity was identified with humanity, Rauschenbusch expressed, and in God we live and in us God dwells, though God's being transcends ours. Therefore, man and woman's sins against the least of their fellow human beings concern God. People do not sin against a remote God, but God feels the thrust of their sinful blows within the commonwealth of humanity. Concerning the criticism against the social gospel for preaching sin in the plural and not just in the singular sense, Rauschenbusch said, "I sometimes believe that the devil lies back in his pew and smiles at our attacks in the abstract; what he gets restless about is the talk about particular sins."[38]

Rauschenbusch realized that the only adequate method for humanity to measure sin was in contrast to righteousness. In this way individuals would acquire the proper hate and repugnance for it. He envisioned the positive ideals of social righteousness in the person of Jesus Christ and in the Kingdom of God. It is Christ who convicts the world of sin.

> Men have made of Jesus a pivot of doctrine. They needed his incarnation and death as the basis of redemption in theology, but they have not always caught the tremendous social energy of righteousness which he embodied. We are a little afraid of his teachings of the Church. I am a respectable man; I have no vices; so far as the Church is concerned it "has nothing on me." But when it comes to the moral demands of Jesus I step out, I am smitten with conviction of sin when he applies his standard to me.[39]

Only the person who has been convicted of sin by Christ and who has a clear vision of the Kingdom of God will have a clear realization of the nature of sin. The chief significance of the social gospel for the doctrine of sin, Rauschenbusch thought, was to revive the vision of the Kingdom of God. When the world in which humanity is living is measured by the Kingdom, the ideal person is able to see clearly the contrast between the reign of organized evil and the reign of organized righteousness. The realization of the Kingdom of God will be found in a reign of love and a commonwealth of labor. "Sin," Rauschenbusch said, "is the greatest preacher of repentance. Give it time, and it will cool our lust in shame.... Mammonism stands convicted by its own works."[40]

Original Sin

Original sin was the concept that Rauschenbusch used to show the transmission of sin from generation to generation. He saw that many theologians were ready to abandon the doctrine of original sin and that laity had begun to ridicule its usage. But Rauschenbusch saw a depth of reality in the old doctrine.

I take pleasure, therefore, in defending it. It is one of the few attempts of individualistic theology to get a solidaristic view of its field of work. This doctrine views the race as a great unity, descended from a single head, and knit together through all ages by unity of origin and blood. This natural unity is the basis and carrier for the transmission and universality of sin. Depravity of will and corruption of nature are transmitted wherever life itself is transmitted.[41]

Rauschenbusch, however, did not treat the doctrine of the fall in the traditional manner. "The older theology had the doctrine of the fall as a cornerstone of the whole structure; here Rauschenbusch," D. R. Sharpe observes, "is an iconoclast."[42] The biblical story of the fall, Rauschenbusch related, will not bear the tremendous weight placed on it by the theological system of the past. The original purpose of the story was not to explain the origin of sin as traditional theology taught, but to show the origin of death and evil. Traditional theology had overworked the doctrine of original sin and tried to involve all humankind in the guilt of Adam as well as in his debasement of nature and in his punishment of death. This, Rauschenbusch continued, fixed on all humanity a uniform corruption that was made so complete that the evil resulting from one's personal sins was naïve and irrelevant.[43]

Rauschenbusch, by using biblical criticism, observed that the story of the fall is considered more fundamental in later theology than it was in the Bible itself. Genesis 3, he noted, was a portion of the "Jahvist" narrative that is dated in the ninth century BC. The prophets were deeply conscious of sin, but their teaching was not based on the doctrine of the fall. The Old Testament makes scarcely any allusions to the story, and it is not until one examines the post-biblical Jewish theology that any general interest is found in Adam's fall. In the synoptic sayings of Jesus, Rauschenbusch did not find any reference to the fall of Adam, while in the fourth Gospel he found only one allusion, John 8:44.[44]

Rauschenbusch was not averse to using biblical criticism and stated his position on the teaching of "higher criticism" by Baptist professors in a response he made in 1896 to the controversy.

> Baptists have no authoritative creeds to which we pledge the teachers of our churches. We have never put the future under bond to the past. In taking the Bible as our standard, we have taken . . . the record of a continuous and progressive unfolding of the truth. . . . Even if some of us do not belong to it ourselves, we assert the right of a liberal wing of the Baptist denomination to exist and to contribute its share to our development.[45]

Paul, Rauschenbusch thought, was the chief exponent of the story of the fall in the Bible. This was seen in Paul's interpretation of the carnal nature of humanity that he saw as descended from Adam and in contrast to the spiritual humanity that descended to man/woman from Christ. Rauschenbusch accepted these passages (Romans 5 and 1 Corinthians 15) as belonging to the theological portion of Paul's writings and felt that they were so difficult that even the modern methods of exegesis had not made Paul's meaning certain.[46] The texts that were usually quoted in support of the doctrine of the fall, Rauschenbusch stated, could not be justly made to have such universal significance.[47]

Rauschenbusch had no difficulty in dealing with the authority of the Pauline passages because to him Jesus was the final word of authority for Christian minds. He observed that in later times, the doctrine of inspiration had neutralized the peculiar position of Jesus and he ranked other writings of the Bible on the same level of inspired infallibility. "I believe that we ought to go back to the apostolic practice and rank Jesus above all others."[48] Simply because Paul's writings composed a large bulk of the New Testament did not necessarily mean that his views were those generally prevailing in the apostolic age. Therefore, Rauschenbusch affirmed that "Paul was a radical in theology, but a social conservative."[49] He went so far as to say that he did not think that Paul even believed in social Christianity.[50]

In Rauschenbusch's opinion, theology had been mistaken in placing such basic importance on the doctrine of the fall, to which Jesus and the prophets had given little or no attention. The only biblical writer to give the story religious importance, he observed, was Paul, and even to him it was not as central as the antagonism between spirit and flesh. Therefore, Rauschenbusch concluded, the traditional doctrine of the fall is mainly the product of speculative interest, and it does not have the preponderance of authority that it once exercised.[51]

Theology had tried to reveal the nature of sin by presenting a contrast between the sinless condition of Adam before the fall and his sinful condition after it. Rauschenbusch objected to this for two reasons. First, Christian theology had tried to convert Adam into a perfect Christian, but no one was able to know whether Adam was as perfect as he is portrayed. In the second place, the Christian cannot derive his interpretation of sin from Adam because Adam's situation gave limited opportunities for selfishness, which is the essence of sin. The solitariness of Adam gave theology a fatal departure toward an individualistic doctrine of sin.[52] Rauschenbusch summed up his position in one sentence: "It is Christ who convicts the world of sin and not Adam."[53]

Rauschenbusch conceived of the social gospel as above all things practical. It needs religious ideas that will release energy for heroic opposition against organized evil and for the building of a righteous social life. It would find entire satisfaction in the attitude of Jesus and the prophets, who dealt with sin as a present force and did not find it necessary to indoctrinate men on its first origin. It would have no motive to be interested in a doctrine that diverts attention from the active factors of sin that can be influenced and concentrates attention on a past event that no efforts of ours can influence.[54]

Traditional theology had presented the fall as an event so complete in the past that sins by our recent forefathers and foremothers were of little consequence. But Rauschenbusch felt that some blame should be reserved for them since they had corrupted us with syphilis, graft, wars, debts, despotic churches, and unbelievable creeds. The doctrine of the fall had done severe damage by its concept of total depravity and had obstructed man and woman's consciousness of their real involvement in sin.[55] The social gospel of Rauschenbusch called for an awakening from the sleep imposed by the dead Adamic dogma of individualism.

But Rauschenbusch saw that there was a substance of truth in the doctrine of original sin. Theology had been correct in emphasizing the biological transmission of evil on the basis of racial solidarity, and Rauschenbusch felt that science, to a degree, supported this concept.

> Evil does flow down the generations through the channels of biological coherence. Idiocy, and feeble-mindedness, neurotic disturbances, weakness of inhibition, perverse desires, stubbornness and anti-social impulses in children must have had their adequate biological causes somewhere back on the line, even if we lack the records.[56]

Rauschenbusch's doctrine of original sin was a social concept. Traditional theology, he felt, had overlooked the fact that sin was transmitted along the lines of social tradition and assimilation as well as by biological propagation.

> The permanent vices and crimes of adults are not transmitted by heredity, but by being socialized; for instance, alcoholism and all drug evils; cruel sports . . . . Just as syphilitic corruption is forced on helpless fetus in its mother's womb, so these hereditary social evils are forced on the individual embedded in the womb of society and drawing his ideas, moral standards, and spiritual ideals from the general life of the social body.[57]

Rauschenbusch was concerned with much more than just the influence of evil examples. He was concerned with the spiritual authority exercised by society over its members. This view grew out of his concept of the nature of sin. No person sins alone, but all of humankind is involved in the solidarity of evil. "This view of original sin," Vernon P. Bodein states, "is opposed to any too liberal belief in the inherent goodness of the human race."[58] Rauschenbusch observed that to a large extent the moral judgments of individuals were shaped and determined by the societal image. If society approved of certain actions, man and woman indulged freely, but when the societal image bore the badge of disapproval, a person's actions were greatly restrained. The profitableness and idealization of evil by society has been an indispensable means of its perpetuation.[59] Rauschenbusch gave the use of alcohol as an example to show the power of the societal image. Certain drug habits such as the use of opium, cocaine, or heroin are condemned by society and so are engaged in secret and shame. Why does the alcohol habit flourish openly? Social authority! The economic forces push it openly, and drinking is praised in song and poetry as a source for entertainment and pleasure. As long as evil is profitable and is idealized by the societal image, the individual will find one's path toward righteousness greatly obscured by powerful social forces.

Niebuhr has stated that Rauschenbusch's view of the transmission of evil through social institutions has placed the responsibility of evil outside and never inside a particular will and is "thus virtually identical with the modern secular idea of the 'cultural lag' as the explanation of evil in human actions."[60] This seems to be an unjust criticism in light of Rauschenbusch's definition of the nature of sin. Since sin is basically selfishness and rebellion against God, it arises out of man and woman's will for self-assertion. Rauschenbusch's statement that "by our very nature we are involved in tragedy"[61] was cited earlier, but he also raised a question as to the degree of humanity's "tragedy." "If our will is so completely depraved, where do we get the freedom on which alone responsibility can be based?"[62] Also, the question needs to be asked whether one can say that sin must necessarily arise only from within one's being. Schleiermacher has said that "we are conscious of sin partly as having its source in ourselves, partly as having its source outside our own being."[63] Rauschenbusch seems to have been influenced by Schleiermacher here, for he saw the source of sin not only within one's personal selfishness but also lodged in social customs and institutions. Therefore, Rauschenbusch does not believe that man or woman is a lone individual responsible only for his or her private sins. Every individual is involved with humanity in sin, and the power and authority of the social group perpetuates the transmission of sin along the lines of social tradition and assimilation.

William E. Hordern also criticized Rauschenbusch for failing to see sin as a part of a person's very being and stated that Rauschenbusch retained pelagian tendencies.[64] Whether Hordern is correct in asserting that Rauschenbusch had pelagian tendencies is difficult to say, but one thing is obvious. Rauschenbusch's concept of original sin was definitely not in the Augustinian tradition. The social view of the transmission of sin, Rauschenbusch thought, offered a better corrective against sin than the traditional biological concept.

> There is the more inducement to teach clearly on the social transmission and perpetuation of sin because the ethical and religious forces can really do something to check and prevent the transmission of original sin, whereas the biological transmission of original sin, except for the possible influence of eugenics, seems to be beyond influence.[65]

The Kingdom of Evil

Rauschenbusch had no naïve view of the advance of the Kingdom of God. He knew that it would come only by "conflict with hostile forces which resist, neutralize, and defy whatever works toward the true social order."[66] He stated that Christ had recognized this conflict and had accepted the fight for himself and called all his disciples to accept their share in the war against evil. The great social problem for Christ was redemption from evil, and he knew that every advance toward the Kingdom of God had to be won by conflict.[67] "His attack is by the truth; whoever is won by that, is conquered for good. Force merely changes the form of evil. When we 'overcome evil with good,' we eliminate it."[68]

Personal Sin

Although Rauschenbusch's chief emphasis was on the corporate involvement of humanity in sin, he was in no way trying to obscure or obliterate responsibility for personal sin. "The A B C of social renewal and moral advance is for each of us to face our sins sincerely and get on a basis of frankness with God and ourselves," he argued. "Therefore, Christianity set out with a call for personal repentance."[69]

Therefore, Rauschenbusch did not begin with an effacement of individual responsibility but affirmed that it was humanity's "most obvious duty . . . to clean up his own backyard and repent of his sins."[70] He had seen that it was impossible for an individual to help others see the validity of the social gospel until she herself was free from the spell that blinded her to her own sinfulness. The first requirement of the social gospel, as in individualistic religion, is to repent and believe in the gospel.[71]

> As we stand before God, we realize that we have loaded up our life with debts we can never pay. We have wasted our time, and the powers of body and soul. We have left black marks of contagion on some whose path we have crossed. We have hurt even those who loved us by our ill-temper, thoughtlessness, and selfishness. We can only ask God to forgive and give us another chance: "Forgive us our debts."[72]

According to Rauschenbusch, the nature of sin is essentially selfishness, and as long as this power continues to dominate a person's life, her relationship to God is thwarted. Speaking out forcefully against the sin of "man's inhumanity to man," he declared, "Whoever utilizes a woman to satisfy his desires, without respecting her soul and her equal human worth, prostitutes her," he declared. "Whoever utilizes a man to satisfy his desire for wealth, without respecting his soul and his equal human worth, and without realizing the beating heart and hopes of his fellow, prostitutes him."[73]

From the prayers of Rauschenbusch, one is able to discern clearly the great power that he saw sin exerting over the lives of individuals and the devastation it often brought in interpersonal relations.

> O Thou whose light is about me and within me and to whom all things are present, help me this day to keep my life pure in thy sight. Suffer me not by any lawless act of mine to befoul any innocent life or add to the shame and hopelessness of any erring one that struggles faintly against sin. . . . May no reckless word or wonton look from me kindle the slow fires of wayward passion that will char and consume the divine beauties of any soul. Give me grace to watch over the imaginations of my heart, lest in the unknown hour of my weakness my secret thoughts leap into action and my honor be turned into shame.[74]

In the concluding prayer in his book, *Prayers of the Social Awakening*, Rauschenbusch in realization of his own sinful weakness prayed, "Pardon the frailty of thy servant, and look upon him only as he sinks his life in Jesus, his Master and Saviour."[75] Bodein has attested to the recognition of individual sin in Rauschenbusch's concept and stated that "Rauschenbusch does full justice to the distinction between the deliberate choice of evil and other forms of social evil."[76] Bodein does remark, however, that Rauschenbusch was not as clear in his use of language on this concept as he might have been.[77]

Extensive quotations have been given from the writings of Rauschenbusch to reveal his emphasis on man and woman's personal sins. Man/Woman was indeed involved with humanity in a corporate sense, but Rauschenbusch saw that a man or woman's step into the Kingdom of God could only come by awareness of one's sinful nature that came from a confrontation with the living Spirit of God and resulted in personal repentance.

Collective Sin

Rauschenbusch had not obliterated a person's responsibility for his or her personal sins, but his primary concern was that every person realizes a corporate involvement in sin. The nature of sin was seen not simply as a private matter between an individual and God but as a solidaristic concept that unified humankind in common involvement in the Kingdom of Evil. "The life of humanity is infinitely interwoven, always renewing itself, yet always perpetuating what has been," he wrote. "The evils of one generation are caused by the wrongs of the generations that preceded, and will in turn condition the sufferings and temptations of those who come after."[78]

Rauschenbusch seemed to have been greatly influenced by Schleiermacher and Ritschl in his solidaristic conception of sin. He quoted from Ritschl, showing the attestation that this great mind gave to the idea of the corporate nature of humanity: "The consciousness of solidarity is one of the fundamental conditions of religion, without which it can neither be rightly understood nor rightly lived."[79] Rauschenbusch enumerated Schleiermacher's concept of the racial sin in the following passage: "Sinfulness . . . is something wholly common

THE DOCTRINE OF SIN

to us . . . not pertaining to every individual separately or referring to him alone, but *in each the work of all, and in all the work of each* [Rauschenbusch's italics]."[80]

The comprehensive view of the corporate nature of humanity quickly shatters any pretensions of self-righteousness and calls for a growing sense of responsibility for the common sin of humanity in which all share and to which all contribute.[81] Society was seen by Rauschenbusch as being so integral that when one person sinned, others suffered also, and when one social class sinned, the whole community suffered the consequences brought by that sin.[82] He conceived of the ideal society as an "organism,"[83] and he viewed Paul's concept of the church as the body of Christ as "the first and classical discussion in Christian thought of the nature and functioning of a composite spiritual organism."[84] God was seen as the bond of racial unity, and all our life found its expression of solidarity from our common basis in God.[85] From this viewpoint, man/woman is not merely an atomistic individual but is also an intricate participant within the commonwealth of humanity.

Individualistic theology in the opinion of Rauschenbusch had greatly erred in not recognizing super-personal forces of evil. In his concept of original sin, he noted that sin was transmitted partially through social forces, and so the social gospel had come to realize the importance and power of super-personal forces and was striving to keep them from becoming parasitic and oppressive.[86] Rauschenbusch's concept of super-personal forces was derived from Josiah Royce, and the following passage revealed his indebtedness to Royce.

> There are in the human world two profoundly different grades, or levels, of mental beings,—namely, the beings that we usually call human individuals, and the beings that we call communities.—Any highly organized community is as truly a human being as you and I are individually human . . . . Yet there are reasons for attributing to a community a mind of its own . . . . Their mental existence is no mere creation of abstract thinking or of metaphor; and is no more a topic for mystical insight, or for phantastic speculation, than is the mental existence of an individual man.[87]

Rauschenbusch saw these super-personal entities as powerful forces of evil and felt that unless they were adequately considered in theology, the concepts of sin and redemption would be unrelated to some of the most important work of redemption.[88] In his opinion, the corporate evil entities had usually fallen from a higher position. The organizations were not thought of as being formed for specific evil purposes, except in rare instances, but had drifted into evil because of need, temptation, or sinister leadership.[89] He called for the redemption of social evil as well as the conversion of individuals within the social evil group. But he saw that it was a much more complicated matter when evil was socialized. His discussion about the familiar boy's gang was one method he used to elucidate the solidarity of the social group for good or evil over its members. He pointed out that it was not enough to win individual boys away from the gang. He believed that the gang spirit itself needed to be Christianized so that it would no longer be a force for evil but one used to restrain and stimulate its members for good.[90]

Religious interest, Rauschenbusch observed, had been so focused on individualistic sin that it had almost completely overlooked the super-personal entities. He saw the chief exceptions to this in the solidaristic concept that the Old Testament prophets had of Israel as a corporate personality, the nature of the family, and the church as a spiritual organism.[91] When the composite personalities in society become combinations for evil, the power of sin is greatly intensified.

In Rauschenbusch's thought, the solidaristic spiritual concept of sin converges in the doctrine of the Kingdom of Evil. Using an analogy of the sheep tick who hides in the wool of the sheep and taps the sheep's blood, Rauschenbusch pointed out that human ticks had acquired control of legislation, courts, police, military, royalty, the church, property, and religion and had gone to the extreme of making alterations in national constitutions in order that the "tick class" might live in greater comfort and bliss. The modern social gospel calls this the Kingdom of Evil.[92] Rauschenbusch's whole book *Christianizing the Social Order* was a message about sin and salvation that dealt searchingly with the great collective sins of his age.[93] He felt that any doctrine of sin was fragmentary unless it saw "all men in their natural

THE DOCTRINE OF SIN

groups bound together in a solidarity of all times and all places, bearing the yoke of evil and suffering."[94] The only influence he saw that could renew the concept of the Kingdom of Evil was the social gospel. It alone had an adequate view of the solidarity of humanity and a sufficient understanding of the social realities of sin.[95]

Satanology

The problem of evil was evidently a powerful thorn in the mind of Rauschenbusch. He had wrestled with this acute problem in all his works. At Rochester he had taught a course on "The Devil" in which he studied the history of the personalized concept of the principle of evil showing its origins, developments, and personal and social consequences.[96] He observed that there was more involved in the concept of sin than merely our own frailty and stupidity and the bad influence of others, but that there existed a permanent force of organized evil. He wrote, "The belief in a satanic power of evil expresses the conviction of the permanent power of evil."[97]

Rauschenbusch saw little evidence in the Old Testament for a belief in the satanic kingdom until after the exile. Persian dualism had deeply affected later Judaism, and after the exile a systematized belief in a satanic kingdom was rampant. This belief in satanic forces was transferred from Judaism to Christianity and was considered part of the essence of Christianity by the early Church Fathers.[98] The authority of the Mediaeval Church established an elaborate systematization of the satanic kingdom based on popular superstition and undergirded with speculative theology. Rauschenbusch enumerated how the church had moved from an offensive into a defensive position in the following account:

> The Christian spirit was thrown into an attitude of defense only. The best that could be done was to hold the powers of darkness at bay by the sign of the cross, by holy water, by sacred amulet, by prayer, by naming holy names. The church buildings and church yards were places of refuge from which the evil spirits were banned. The gargoyles of Gothic architecture are the evil spirits escaping

from the church building because the spiritual power within is unbearable to them.[99]

Rauschenbusch noted that the reformation leaders had made no attack on the belief in a demonic kingdom and that Protestantism as well as Catholicism had helped its continuation. Thomas Aquinas had provided the satanic concept with a theological basis while the Inquisition had reduced it to practice. The bull *Summis desiderantes* gave the concept the church's highest authority in 1484 by Innocent VIII, and in the *Malleus Maleficarum* it became codified and was a part of orthodoxy.[100] "If the devil and his spirits are not real but a figment of social imagination, yet at that time the devil was real . . . . Theology had made him real."[101] But now, Rauschenbusch observed, the belief in a satanic kingdom exists only where theological tradition keeps it alive, and this is confined usually to premillennialists or conservative church groups.

In Rauschenbusch's opinion, Satan and his devils were a fading religious entity, and the Kingdom of Evil could no longer be considered a demonic power. He believed that in early Christianity, the belief in Satan was closely connected with the opposition of the Christians to the pagan social order. He elucidated this idea by showing the close alliance in the *Apocalypse* between the dragon who stood for Satan and the beasts who stood for the Roman Empire.[102] Therefore, Rauschenbusch stated, the belief in a satanic kingdom drew its vitality from political and social realities and not from mere theological speculation. Education had dispelled the belief in demonic spirits, but the identification of satanic powers with political and social realities had been diminished and Satan had become merely a theological devil. Rauschenbusch called for a reevaluation of the belief in a satanic kingdom based on political and social protest that had been the purpose of a belief in the satanic kingdom when it had its greatest vitality. He felt that its solidaristic concept of evil needed to be maintained, or humanity would be concerned mainly with transient individualistic sins.[103]

Rauschenbusch thought of the devil not as an abstract evil personality but as a concept used to denote the personification of evil forces. The satanic kingdom was far from being an abstract notion in his thought but was seen as objectified in business, war, tyranny, capitalism, and any force that negated the intrinsic worth of people.

The social gospel of Rauschenbusch had called for a reexamination and expansion of the doctrine of sin. Having examined this doctrine briefly, our attention in the next chapter will be focused on his concept of soteriology, which is a natural theological outworking of his doctrine of sin.

Notes

1. Mary Frances Thelen, *Man as Sinner in Contemporary American Realistic Theology* (Oxford: Kings Crown Press, 1946) 13.

2. H. Richard Niebuhr, *The Kingdom of God in America* (New York: Harper & Brothers, 1937) 192.

3. John C. Bennett, "The Social Interpretation of Christianity," *The Church through Half a Century: Essays in Honor of William Adams Brown*, ed. Samuel Cavert and Henry Van Dusen (New York: Charles Scribner's, 1936) 120–21.

4. Walter Rauschenbusch, *A Theology for the Social Gospel* (New York: Macmillan Company, 1917) 31.

5. Gary J. Dorrien, *Reconstructing the Common Good: Theology and the Social Order* (Maryknoll NY: Orbis Books, 1990) 38.

6. WR, *A Theology for the Social Gospel*, 32–33.

7. Ibid., 32.

8. Ibid., 31–32.

9. Ibid., 36.

10. Ibid., 35.

11. Ibid., 35–36.

12. Ibid., 37.

13. Ibid., 45–46.

14. Ibid., 46–47.

15. Ibid., 47.

16. Ibid.

17. Ibid.

18. In Arnold S. Nash, ed., *Protestant Thought in the Twentieth Century* (New York: Macmillan Company, 1951) 129.

19. In George L. Hunt, ed., *Ten Makers of Modern Protestant Thought* (New York: Association Press, 1958) 37.

20. Charles W. Kegley and Robert W. Bretall, *Reinhold Niebuhr, His Religious, Social, and Political Thought*, vol. 2 of the Library of Living Theology (New York: Macmillan Company, 1956) 358–59.

21. Paul Tillich, *Systematic Theology*, vol. 2 (Chicago: University of Chicago Press, 1957) 50.

22. Ibid., 50–51.

23. Reinhold Niebuhr, *The Nature and Destiny of Man*, 2 vols. (New York: Charles Scribner's Sons, 1949) 1:186.

24. Ibid.

25. Ibid., 187. Niebuhr quoting from Pascal's *Faugère*, vol. 1, 197.

26. WR, *A Theology for the Social Gospel*, 52.

27. Niebuhr, *The Nature and Destiny of Man*, 1:188.

28. Ibid., 228. In Niebuhr's discussion of sin as sensuality, he speaks of selfishness as the "destruction of life's harmony by the self's attempt to centre life around itself. . . ."

29. Hans Hofmann, *The Theology of Reinhold Niebuhr*, trans. Louise P. Smith (New York: Charles Scribner's Sons, 1956) 72.

30. Niebuhr, *The Nature and Destiny of Man*, 1:179. See Niebuhr, *Faith and History* (New York: Charles Scribner's Sons, 1949) 121: "Man is at variance with God through this abortive effort to establish himself as his own Lord; and he is at variance with his fellow men by the force of the same pride which brings him in conflict with God."

31. Richard Dickerson, "Rauschenbusch and Niebuhr: Brothers Under the Skin," *Religion in Life* 27 (Spring 1958): 171.

32. Ibid., 166.

33. George Hammar, *Christian Realism in Contemporary American Theology* (Uppsala: A. B. Lundequistska Bokhandeln, 1940) 157.

34. WR, *A Theology for the Social Gospel*, 5.

35. Ibid., 97.

36. H. Shelton Smith, *Changing Conceptions of Original Sin* (New York: Charles Scribner's Sons, 1955) 202.

37. WR, *A Theology for the Social Gospel*, 48.

38 WR, "The Conservation of the Social Service Message," *Messages of the Men and Religion Movement, Social Service*, vol. 2 (New York: Funk and Wagnalls Company, 1912) 123.

39. WR, "The Social Background, Spirit, and Message of the Bible," *The Rochester Theological Seminary Record*, November 1918, p. 55.

40. WR, *Christianizing the Social Order* (New York: Macmillan Company, 1919) 5.

41. WR, *A Theology for the Social Gospel*, 57–58.

42. Dores R. Sharpe, *Walter Rauschenbusch* (New York: Macmillan Company, 1942) 326.

43. WR, *A Theology for the Social Gospel*, 59.

44. Ibid., 39–40.

45. LeRoy Moore, Jr., "Academic Freedom: A Chapter in the History of the Colgate Rochester Divinity School," *Foundations* 10 (January–March 1967): 67. Quoted in Bill J. Leonard, *Baptist Ways: A History* (Valley Forge: Judson Press, 2003) 398.

46. WR, *A Theology of the Social Gospel*, 59.

47. Ibid. Rauschenbusch listed the following texts that were usually cited as proof of the validity of the doctrine of the fall: Gen 6:5; 8:21; Pss 14:1-3; 51:5; 58:3; Isa 48:8; John 3:5-6; Rom 5:12-14; and Eph 2:3.

48. WR, *The Rochester Theological Seminary Record*, 54.

49. WR, *Christianity and the Social Crisis* (New York: Macmillan Company, 1912) 102.

50. Rauschenbusch, *The Rochester Theological Seminary Record*, 62. See Holmes Rolston, *The Social Message of the Apostle Paul* (Richmond: John Knox Press, 1942). Rolston is convinced that Paul had a definite social message and that his message has been unduly neglected by the Christian church.

51. WR, *A Theology for the Social Gospel*, 41–42.

52. Ibid., 51.

53. Ibid., 52.

54. Ibid., 42.

55. Ibid., 42–43.

56. Ibid., 58.

57. Ibid., 60.

58. Vernon P. Bodein, *The Social Gospel of Walter Rauschenbusch and Its Relation to Religious Education* (New Haven: Yale University Press, 1944) 141.

59. WR, *A Theology for the Social Gospel*, 66.

60. Niebuhr, *The Nature and Destiny of Man*, 246.

61. WR, *A Theology for the Social Gospel*, 32.

62. Ibid., 59.

63. Friedrich Schleiermacher, *The Christian Faith*, ed. and trans. H. R. Mackintosh and J. S. Stewart (Edinburgh: T. and T. Clark, 1928) 279.

64. William E. Hordern, "The Theology of the Social Gospel," unpublished Master of Theology thesis, Union Theological Seminary, New York, 1946, p. 18.

65. WR, *A Theology for the Social Gospel*, 67–68.

66. Walter Rauschenbusch, *The Social Principles of Jesus* (New York: Association Press, 1916) 151.

67. Ibid., 158. See WR, *Christianizing the Social Order*, 102.

68. Ibid., 157.

69. Ibid., 81.

70. Ibid., 89.

71. WR, *Christianity and the Social Crisis*, 349–50.

72. WR, *The Social Principles of Jesus*, 151–52.

73. WR, *Dare We Be Christians* (Boston: Pilgrim Press, 1914) 45.

74. WR, *Prayers of the Social Awakening* (Boston: Pilgrim Press, 1909) 103.

75. Ibid.

76. Bodein, *The Social Gospel of Walter Rauschenbusch*, 136.

77. Ibid.

78. WR, *A Theology for the Social Gospel*, 79.

79. Ibid., 94. Rauschenbusch quoting Albrecht Ritschl's *Rechtfertigung und Veröhnung*, vol. 1, 555.

80. Ibid., 92–93. Translated and quoted by Rauschenbusch from Schleiermacher's *The Christian Faith* (pp. 287–89 in Mackintosh and Stewart's English translation).

81. Ibid., 91. See WR, *The Social Principles of Jesus*, 22.

82. Ibid., 182.

83. WR, *Christianizing the Social Order*, 366.

84. WR, *A Theology for the Social Gospel*, 70.

85. Ibid., 184.

86. Ibid., 15.

87. Ibid., 70–71, Rauschenbusch quoting Josiah Royce's *The Problem of Christianity*, vol. 1, 164–67.

88. Ibid., 75–76.

89. Ibid., 72.

90. WR, *The Social Principles of Jesus*, 160.

91. WR, *A Theology for the Social Gospel*, 81.

92. Ibid., 80–81.

93. WR, *Christianizing the Social Order*, ix.

94. WR, *A Theology for the Social Gospel*, 81.

95. Ibid., 87.

96. Sharpe, *Walter Rauschenbusch*, 182.

97. WR, *The Social Principles of Jesus*, 155.

98. WR, *A Theology for the Social Gospel*, 82–83.

99. Ibid., 83.

100. Ibid., 84.

101. Ibid.

102. WR, *The Social Principles of Jesus*, 155.

103. WR, *A Theology for the Social Gospel*, 87–88.

Chapter 5

The Concept of Personal Salvation

The concept of soteriology is always at the heart of the Christian message. Since Rauschenbusch's view of personal salvation has been neglected by many, a reaffirmation of this concept will provide fresh insight into his thought. This chapter will examine his concept of personal salvation in the following aspects: the sacredness and worth of human personality; the relationship of the atonement to the individual; and the influence of the solidaristic comprehension of humanity on individual salvation. Then we will consider a brief examination of the problems of mysticism, asceticism, and immortality that Rauschenbusch saw emanating from an individualistic concept of salvation.

The Sacredness of Personality

In 1913 Shailer Mathews stated, "I think, too, that Professor Rauschenbusch is inclined to minimize the worth of the individual."[1] This statement does not seem to be justifiable, however, for Rauschenbusch had a deep and profound concept of the sacredness and worth of human personality. "True Christianity emphasizes to the utmost the value of the individual," he wrote, "and has been the real motive power back of the efforts to secure personal liberty."[2] "The Church has always stood for a high estimate of potential worth of the soul of man," he wrote in another place. "It has always taught that man was made in God's image and that he is destined to share in the holiness and eternal life of God."[3]

In his book *The Social Principles of Jesus*, Rauschenbusch devoted the first chapter to a discussion of the sacred value of human life and personality. The sacredness of human life was seen as an axiomatic social principle in the basic convictions of Jesus.[4] Neither physical deformity nor moral guilt obscured the divine worth of human personality to Jesus. The religious insight into human life and destiny was the cause of the respect Jesus had for all people. The consciousness of a God of love revealed to Jesus the beauty of humanity, and the awareness of God as the great Father revealed people as children of God.[5]

Rauschenbusch asserted that in the Sermon on the Mount, Jesus raised the standard of social morality to a higher level. He put hate and contempt under the same category as murder and stated that when a person abused another with words of contempt, she denied the divine worth of the person and robbed herself of self-respect and the respect of others. "It is an attempt to murder his own soul. The horror which Jesus feels for such action is an expression of his own respect for the worth of personality."[6]

In a speech delivered at the New York State Conference on Religion in 1900, Rauschenbusch enumerated forcefully the supreme value he saw in a human soul: "The souls filled with the life of God are the fountains from which all life-giving impulses flow into the life of society. But a human soul is of eternal value for its own sake, and not merely for the effect it may have on society, just as our children are dear to us apart from any work they may do."[7]

He viewed war and prostitution as the most flagrant distortions of the sacredness of personality. He saw war as a wholesale waster of human life and recognized prostitution as a form of utter contempt for the worth of personality.[8] In Rauschenbusch's opinion, Jesus did not speak about eliminating the unfit but about saving them and lifting them up to a new standard of living. This required a greater constructive energy and a greater faith in the dormant capacities of human personality. Jesus did not attempt to weaken or suppress human personality, but wherever he went his spirit was an awakening force and an emancipator for the downcast in society.[9] Quoting Wilhelm Wundt, Rauschenbusch said that "humanity in the highest sense was brought into the world by Christianity."[10]

To Rauschenbusch the social concern of Christianity would be in a state of impoverishment without the conception of the sacredness of human personality, and he urged all who would duplicate the spirit of Jesus to have always a loving regard for human life. "That sense of sacredness is the basis for the whole missionary and philanthropic activity of Christian men and women," he insisted.[11] Reverence for personality affirmed that a person would never be treated only as a means, but always as an end in one's self. He stated that there always had to be the realization of the divine worth in every person.

Quoting Henry C. King, Rauschenbusch summed up his concept of the sacredness of the human personality in the following manner:

> The principle of reverence for personality is the ruling principle in ethics, and in religion; it constitutes, therefore, the truest and highest test of either an individual or a civilization; it has been even unconsciously, the guiding and determining principle in all human progress; and in its religious interpretation, it is, indeed, the one faith that keeps meaning and value for life.[12]

The Individual and the Atonement

Many have accused Rauschenbusch of not having a substantial concept of personal salvation. A. T. Robertson presented a typical example of these accusations when he said, "At times one suspects that he [Rauschenbusch] almost merged Christianity into the 'New Social Order' at the expense of the personal experience of grace."[13] Even as late as 2007, Tony Campolo still accused Rauschenbusch of not asserting the need for personal conversion in a transforming way with Christ.[14] In his foreword to the one-hundredth-anniversary edition of his great-grandfather's first book, Paul Raushenbush observed that conservative evangelicals such as Rick Warren wrote that "Rauschenbusch was a liberal theologian and he basically said that we don't need this stuff about Jesus anymore."[15] Douglas Weaver has rightly interpreted Rauschenbusch when he wrote that the man "did not reject the traditional gospel call for personal conversion, but he added the biblical mandate for social salvation."[16]

Rauschenbusch's primary emphasis was on social redemption, and all his books resounded with that emphasis. But underlying his social concern was his concept of personal redemption. Humanity's responsibility for personal sins had not been obliterated by individuals, however, and he stated that "Christianity set out with a call for personal repentance."[17] Because a person was personally involved in sin, he saw that every person's confrontation with God was likewise personal: "True Christianity puts a man face to face with Christ and bids him see what he can find there."[18] Rauschenbusch decried those who would mistake social action for authentic Christian faith. "We do not want to substitute social activities for religion," he wrote. "If the church comes to lean on social preachings and doings as a crutch because its religion has become paralytic, may the Lord have mercy on us all."[19] In *The Righteousness of the Kingdom*, published after his death in 1968, Rauschenbusch stated the truth that he affirmed in many places: "A man is saved according as he enters or does not enter the Kingdom."[20]

In Rauschenbusch's concept of human life, there were two great entities; one was the human soul and the other was the human race. The purpose of religion was to save both. The soul was to seek righteousness and eternal life, while the human race was to look for righteousness and the Kingdom of God.[21] Rauschenbusch put his chief emphasis on the corporate aspect of salvation because he felt that the individualistic aspect of redemption was being propagated to the neglect of the social implications. However, he did not overlook the necessity for every person's experiential encounter with God. He affirmed that "the salvation of the individual is, of course, an essential part of salvation. Every new being is a new problem of salvation."[22] In an address on "The History of the Idea of the Kingdom of God," delivered before the students and faculty of the German Department of Rochester Theological seminary on September 12, 1902, Rauschenbusch stated that "the individual is a permanent fact in God's universe, and the salvation of one single soul from selfishness and carnal living unto spiritual life and serving love is a growth of the Kingdom of God."[23]

To Rauschenbusch, spiritual regeneration was the most important fact that any person could experience in her own life history, and this personal experience was of supreme value for its own sake.

> A living experience of God is the crowning knowledge attainable to a human mind. Each one of us needs the redemptive power of religion for his own sake, for on the tiny stage of the human soul all the vast world tragedy of good and evil is reenacted. In the best social order that is conceivable men will still smolder with lust and ambition, and be lashed by hate and jealousy as with the whip of a slave driver. No material comfort and plenty can satisfy the restless soul in us and give us peace with ourselves. All who have made test of it agree that religion alone holds the key to the ultimate meaning of life, and each of us must find his way into the inner mysteries alone. The day will come when all life on this planet will be extinct, and what meaning will our social evolution have had if that is all? Religion is eternal life in the midst of time and transcending time.[24]

Rauschenbusch realized that social reform was impossible without men and women in the societal group who had experienced personal religion. Reform could only come from individuals who had themselves undergone a personal reformation. For this reason he did not endorse the Citizens Movement of 1890 in *For the Right*.

> Some of the men who are in this movement have made great fortunes by notoriously corrupt methods. They are the pillars of that system which we protest against—the system which makes it possible for men to rob their neighbors, and which puts power into the hands of the unscrupulous. We cannot, we will not join hands with any man whose pockets are filled with ill gotten gains, and whose hands are on his brother's throat. Reforms can succeed only when pure men inaugurate them. In the church or out of it, the man who rises upon the prostrate form of his fellow man is a thief and a robber. And can the thief, whether in the church or out of it reform anything? Let us have reform by all means, social, political and religious. But let us have clean men behind the movement.[25]

Rauschenbusch stated that the greatest contribution any person could make to the social movement was a regenerated personality.[26] He acknowledged that "the human soul with its guilt and its longing for holiness and deathless life is a permanent fact in religion, and no social perfection will quench its hunger for the living God."[27] Anyone who has read Rauschenbusch's works carefully can see that he did not expect social reformation to come without first an appeal to the individual soul for repentance and personal faith.[28] He envisioned every "saved soul" as a fulcrum upon which God could rest his lever to turn humanity "right side up."[29] He prayed that every person's life would be centered in God and that it would become worthy of the habitation of the living God: "Make us fit to house the Lord of Glory. May Christ be no homeless wanderer so far as we are concerned, but may he find in us a resting place and a temple."[30] Harlan Beckley, in his book focusing on the legacies of Rauschenbusch, John Ryan, and Reinhold Niebuhr, notes that Rauschenbusch concluded both his books on the social order "with a claim that personal regeneration and voluntary self-sacrifice are necessary" as "practical means for Christianizing the social order."[31]

Rauschenbusch depicted man and woman's salvation as being engendered through personal experience with God and not merely as an assent to a set of propositional truths about Christ, writing, "Thus did God reveal himself to men and give them knowledge of himself; not the cold knowledge of speculation, but the burning, overpowering knowledge of religious experience."[32] True Christianity, he asserted, could never be reduced to a system of doctrinal assertions but always put a person face to face with Christ.

> If salvation were for those who understood a system of truth, salvation would belong to refined brain cells. If Christianity were, as some say, a religion of a book, it would be a religion of the favored classes. But it is not a religion of a book, but of a man, and a man is both the most unfathomable and the simplest object of human knowledge. It requires only a childlike heart, a limpid soul, to understand the revelation of God in Christ.[33]

Rauschenbusch expressed the belief that the culminating revelation of God was objectified in a historical event. "When God revealed himself," Rauschenbusch stated, "it was not by communicating abstract propositions or systems of doctrine. The fundamental fact in the Christian revelation was that the Word became flesh. Therewith

Truth became History."³⁴ In his opinion no one was able to recognize Jesus as the Christ by instruction or hearsay. This insight could come only by revelation from God himself. "Is it too daring to say that all really spiritual light is kindled by God himself? . . . Are we then not dependent on God for the light of God, which is one aspect of salvation?"³⁵ But Rauschenbusch did not feel that the religious community had no obligation in helping to provide an atmosphere for the working of God's spirit. This he stated clearly in an article on "The Rights of Children in the Community":

> The child has a right to education. We need not lose any words at that point. . . . This brings us close to religious education. We cannot furnish the child its own intimate discovery of God. The wind bloweth where it listeth. We must leave that to God Himself, but we can introduce the child to the religious stories, the history, the hymns, the tales of religious heroism, the atmosphere of reverence and aspiration, which have come down through the various channels of tradition and which constitute the choicest heritage of the race. If left to itself, the child may have some sense of the sublime underneath the starlit skies; it may have groping longings for a pure and holy life; but the religious community can help it to incomparably greater clearness of vision, to a surer sense of the reality and the nearness of God, and to a greater ease and comfort in finding Him and leaning on Him. Religion is the most intimately personal attainment; yet it is mediated to us by the community of those who have it.³⁶

Rauschenbusch asserted that every person needed a great faith that would saturate one's whole life and master one's subconscious mind as well as one's conscious energies. This great faith would lift a person out of the narrow confinement of thought and make that person an inspired instrument of God. Rauschenbusch saw the transformation in Paul's life as evidence of a new faith that had seized him and made him over and brought him to the realization that a person was justified by faith rather than by anything he might do himself.³⁷

One of the great values Rauschenbusch saw in the Reformation was the defacement of the idea that man or woman might be able to "merit" his or her salvation. Christ alone was seen to have merit, and by his death the debt had been paid once and for all. When a person saw that she was unable to earn merit, the contract labor system in religion was ended, and then one needed only to believe and accept the great transaction that had been made on her behalf.[38] "The saints and their intercession were dismissed, they never had any merit either; the sinner could deal with God and Christ direct."[39] Rauschenbusch saw in Jesus the "real revelation of God" and affirmed that union with God could be attained only through him and by his mediation.[40]

In a series of articles titled "Why I Am a Baptist," Rauschenbusch set forth one of his clearest statements on the necessity of experiential religion. He said that "when we Baptists insist on personal experience as the only essential thing in religions, we are hewing our way back to original Christianity."[41] He interpreted the insistence of Baptists on personal experience as freeing men and women from any need of sacramentalism or dogmatism. Faith in Christ was seen as a spiritual experience and was to be necessarily free and voluntary. Someone might be able to compel attendance to a mass or subscription to a creed, but an inner experience can never be compelled; it always has to be free and spontaneous. Rauschenbusch stated that it took a trained mind to understand the fine distinctions of the church creeds and a large amount of historical information to understand the ritual and symbols of some churches, but an experience of God, he affirmed, is open to the simplest mind, even to a little child.[42]

The first reason Rauschenbusch gave for being a Baptist reveals vividly his concept of experiential religion.

> The Christian faith as Baptists hold it sets spiritual experience boldly to the front as the one great thing in religions. It aims at experimental religion. We are an evangelistic body. We summon all men to conscious repentance from sin, to conscious prayer for forgiveness. We ask a man: "Have you put your faith in Christ? Have you submitted your will to His will? Have you received the inward assurance that your sins are forgiven and that you are at peace with God? Have you had experience of God?"
>
> If anyone desires to enter our churches we ask for evidence of such experience and we ask for nothing else. We do not ask him to

recite a creed or catechism. The more simple and heartfelt the testimony is, the better we like it. If it is glib and wordy, we distrust it. Experience is our sole requisite for receiving baptism; it is fundamental in our church life."[43]

In a letter to L. C. Barnes dated May 10, 1918, Rauschenbusch said, "I have always regarded my public work as a form of evangelism, which called for a deeper repentance and a new experience of God's salvation."[44] Few, if any, would regard Rauschenbusch's work as evangelism, yet this was the manner in which he wished to be regarded. Sharpe devoted a chapter in his biography to Rauschenbusch as "The Evangelist," and stated that Rauschenbusch said he had always wanted his work to be thought of as a form of evangelism.[45] Rauschenbusch did not want personal evangelism to be superseded by social redemption, for he felt that nothing could "supersede that great experience when the soul of man consciously turns to God."[46] His earlier interest in evangelical Christianity can be seen in the church hymnal he published with W. Appel in 1889, titled *Neue Lieder*. Among the twelve hymns Rauschenbusch translated for the hymnal were such evangelical ones as "Jesus Saves," "Let the Saviour In," "At the Cross," and "Calvary."[47] Donald Meyer felt that the continuing import of the evangelical religion for the thought of Rauschenbusch was so strong that Rauschenbusch "wished to 'add on' the social gospel to the evangelical personal gospel."[48]

I do not feel that one can justifiably call Rauschenbusch a "conservative evangelical," but one can conceivably consider him an "evangelical liberal." Rauschenbusch's writings in no manner of speaking put the main emphasis on personal salvation, but neither do they attempt to obliterate the significance of a personal religious experience with God. The personal religious life of Rauschenbusch substantiated his belief in the necessity and importance of a personal religious experience. He stated once that "my life would seem an empty shell if my personal religion were left out of it."[49] Sharpe expressed the conviction that "Rauschenbusch's view of religion was born of a deep personal experience of the living God in his own heart and life."[50] Henry B.

Robins has aptly characterized the religious spirit of Rauschenbusch in the following statement:

> He would have disclaimed sainthood in the conventional sense, and none of us, I suppose, ever thought of him in that character, yet among those whose personal Christianity made a lasting impression upon us, he was second to none and holds a place uniquely his own. There was a rare simplicity about his personal approach to God and a passionate yearning for genuine kinship of spirit and experience with Jesus Christ which suffused his whole bearing with an unfailing quality of reverence.[51]

Solidaristic Comprehension and the Individual

A person does indeed experience God personally, Rauschenbusch felt, but with this experience there always has to be the realization of one's solidaristic involvement with humanity. A person is not merely an atomistic individual in relationship with God; she stands within the commonwealth of humanity. Having defined the nature of sin as selfishness and rebellion against God and having insisted on putting humanity in the picture, Rauschenbusch then affirmed that salvation must be a change that turns a person from self to God and to humanity. Any personal religious experience that does not have in it a relationship to our fellow human beings did not seem to him to be a distinctively Christian experience. "A religious experience is not Christian unless it binds us closer to men and commits us more deeply to the Kingdom of God," he asserted.[52] Richard Rorty, Rauschenbusch's grandson and professor of philosophy at Princeton and other universities, believes that the millenarianism and apocalypticism depicted in the *Left Behind* novels and the emergence of religious individualism since the 1970s reveal a similar struggle that awaits the church and contemporary society. This struggle about the belief in millenarianism and apocalypticism existed in Rauschenbusch's day in the later part of the nineteenth century and the early part of the twentieth century, and he rigorously opposed this theological perspective.[53]

Rauschenbusch had seen the life of humanity as being infinitely interwoven. In a Thanksgiving Day homily, he declared, "The sooner we learn that this is a very small planet and getting smaller every year, and that our welfare is bound up with all other passengers, the better it is for all of us." He saw this not only as a religious matter but also as "a great sociological law and all modern science and all modern progress thunders its amen."[53] The nature of sin was seen not simply as a private matter between a person and God, but as a solidaristic concept that unified humankind in common involvement in the Kingdom of Evil. The spiritual solidarity of humanity was seen as an axiomatic social principle in the mind of Jesus, and therefore complete salvation could be possible only when a person took his place in a divine organism of mutual service in which he would freely coordinate his life with the lives of his fellow men and women in an attitude of unselfish love. Self could no longer be the center of a person's universe, but in some germinal form, salvation had to turn one from a life centered on self to a life of service toward God and other people.[54] "When we submit to God," Rauschenbusch said, "we submit to the supremacy of the common good. Salvation is the voluntary socializing of the soul."[55]

In speaking of the terms used to describe salvation, Rauschenbusch stated that "conversion," or "regeneration" and "sanctification," had to be connected with the Kingdom of God. He felt that the entire meaning of "conversion" and "regeneration" was changed when the Kingdom of God concept disappeared from Christian thought. The change in people was not connected with a change in humanity. He asked the question, if one is converted, to what is he converted? Does our regeneration consist in our "going to heaven"? Rauschenbusch replied that the link between our religious experience and humanity is missing when the Kingdom of God is not present in the concept of redemption.[56] Faith was seen as prophetic vision that launches life toward the unseen future; "It is not so much the endorsement of ideas formulated in the past, as expectancy and confidence in the coming salvation of God."[57]

Faith is indeed an intensely personal matter, but it can never be merely a private matter because no person is ever an isolated ego. J. S. Whale points this out when he says,

> Indeed, the most private act that any man can perform is to die, to go out of life. As long as he is alive at all he cannot and does not live unto himself. Personality is mutual in its very being. For all its sovereign individuality, the self exists only in a community of selves. The lonely Robinson Crusoe is a possible fiction because he begins as a man before becoming a solitary; but the lonely Tarzan of the Apes is an impossible fiction because he begins as solitary before becoming a man. Society is only the aggregate of individual selves, admittedly; yet individual selfhood is achieved only in society.... In short, human life demands to be understood in terms of its two complementary aspects, the individual and the corporate, the part and the whole. Each has to be interpreted in terms of the other.[58]

This was the truth Rauschenbusch was trying to unveil to the minds of men and women. Christianity could never be simply an individual matter and no more; it must always have its external expression in the life and activities of the people who had been captivated by the spiritual experience that had taken place within them.

> Thus the insistence that love to God must have its immediate result and counterpoise in love for men is one of the rudiments of Christian faith and feeling. But that does not exhaust the relations between the love of God and the love of man. The causal relation runs the other way too.... It is by loving men that we enter into a living love for God.[59]

To concentrate only on personal salvation as orthodoxy has done, Rauschenbusch said, is closely akin to selfishness, and all that have been trained in egotistic religion need a conversion to "Christian Christianity." "Our religious individuality must get its interpretation from the supreme fact of social solidarity."[60] Rauschenbusch observed that many of the "saved" individuals in the church were worse after their "conversion" experience than they were before. Some had become more self-centered and self-righteous than they ever had been. He pointed to the Pharisees as an example of men who could become worse because of religion. He deplored the idea that salvation could be reduced to signing a card, shaking hands, or being introduced to an evangelist. The social gospel called for a new concept of personal salvation.[61]

Rauschenbusch had affirmed that the social gospel was the old message of salvation and asked his readers in *A Theology for the Social Gospel* "to take all the familiar experience and truths of personal evangelism and religious nurture for granted in what follows."[62] But he also stated that the new solidaristic comprehension of the social gospel deeply affected one's understanding of personal salvation. The solidaristic involvement of humanity had enlarged and intensified the old message of salvation.

> Other things being equal, a solidaristic religious experience is more distinctively Christian than an individualistic religious experience. To be afraid of hell or purgatory and desirous of a life without pain or trouble in heaven was not in itself Christian. It was self-interest on a higher level. . . . But even in more spiritual forms of conversion, as long as men are wholly intent on their own destiny, they do not necessarily emerge from selfishness. It only changes its form. A Christian regeneration must have an outlook toward humanity and result in a higher social consciousness.[63]

Mysticism

In some forms of Christianity, Rauschenbusch observed that mysticism was regarded as the highest form of sanctification. But he felt that the danger of mysticism was its isolation. An individual soul could concentrate only on God and shut out the world while her own consciousness would be swallowed up in the spirit of God. This experience made one indifferent to the world and caused her to be concerned only with her personal experience with God. "The mystic way to holiness is not through humanity but above it,"[64] and therefore, Rauschenbusch felt that it set aside God's fundamental law of love. "The way of holiness through human fellowship and service is slower and lowlier, but its results are more essentially Christian."[65]

Rauschenbusch did not think that Jesus was a mystic in the sense of one who isolated himself from the world. He acknowledged Jesus as our great example of prayer and intimate personal fellowship with God, but noted that Jesus was engaged by the Kingdom of God idea and therefore set his task in the midst of humanity. The strength Jesus drew from God was actively put forth in this world.[66] Rauschenbusch also felt that Paul offered his great chapter on love in 1 Corinthians as "a counterpoise and antidote" to the danger he saw in mysticism.[67]

In examining the religious experience of Moses, Samuel, Isaiah, Jeremiah, and Paul, Rauschenbusch observed that although each individual's experience was intensely personal, it was not the solitary type in which a soul struggled for its own salvation in order to escape the penalties of sin or to attain perfection and peace only for itself. "All were experienced with a conscious outlook toward humanity."[68] The religious experiences of the prophets were seen also as intimate personal experiences with God; "yet they were not ascetic, not individualistic, not directed toward a future life. They were social, political, solidaristic."[69] Rauschenbusch felt that a person's religious experience must not be reduced only to a theocentric mysticism that enabled him to experience God, but that person needed an anthropocentric mysticism that would enable him to realize the necessity of a proper relationship with his fellow men and women as well as with God.[70]

Asceticism

The asceticism and otherworldliness of ancient and medieval Christianity was regarded by Rauschenbusch as a result of the "Hellenization" of Christianity. He saw Christian asceticism as only a modification of the general feeling of pessimism and repugnance that existed toward the world in those ages. He observed that all of these movements to some extent identified evil with matter and felt that the flesh that clothed the soul was evil and had to be opposed and worn down. Sexual desire was regarded as the chief enemy of ascetic religion, and therefore virginity and celibacy came to be considered as a higher form of Christianity than marriage.[71] This undercut one of the fundamental social institutions, the home, and eventually caused the sterilization of some of the best minds. Rauschenbusch observed that "God alone knows where the race might be today if the natural leaders had not so long been made childless by their own goodness."[72]

Asceticism and monasticism were seen as two of the major factors for the failure of Christianity to undertake social reconstruction. Many of the finest individuals were taken out of society and placed in communities by themselves, isolated from the rest of society. "The energy which they ought to have devoted to making society normal, they employed in making themselves abnormal."[73] Rauschenbusch declared that every monastery served as a concrete assertion that the ordinary life of humanity was evil and far removed from Christianity and was also incapable of being Christianized. "Thus the reconstructive aim of Christianity was declared impossible, and the indomitable reconstructive energy of Christianity was turned to the building of ideal communities outside of the common life."[74]

Rauschenbusch felt that any concept of religion that placed its chief emphasis on the salvation of the individual from this world and that involved a negation of this life was unrelated to true Christianity and especially to the life and teaching of Jesus. He could only picture the true follower of Christ as being actively engaged in the Christianizing of the social order and not in seeking an escape from it.

Immortality

In Rauschenbusch's thought, belief in a future life after death was not essential for one to have religious faith. He pointed to the faith of the Old Testament religious leaders and observed that it is doubtful if they believed in a future life, yet they exhibited a rare faith in God. Although he did not see immortality as a self-evident proposition, he felt that a person had a larger and more complete hope if he looked forward to eternal life for himself as well as to a better society in the future history of the race. He saw that the hope of a higher life for the race did not solve the problem for the individual person; and he realized that the best society on earth could not last forever. Therefore, humanity looked for the consummation of one's labors in an existence after death.[75] "A perfect religious hope must include both; eternal life for the individual, the Kingdom of God for humanity."[76]

Faith in a future life, Rauschenbusch felt, had to some extent subdued the demand for social justice. When the hope of eternal life came to the foreground in Christian thought, the Kingdom of God, he noted, receded into the background and with it much of the interest in the social transformation of humanity. The individualistic concept of eternal life was centered on a desire to escape from this world and not to Christianize it.[77] Therefore, he believed that the concept of immortality needed to be Christianized. Salvation to him meant victory over sin rather than escape from hell, and this gave dignity to the present life and not a feeling of weariness toward it. He enumerated his view of Christianizing the concept of eternal life in the following statement:

> It is possible to fear hell and desire heaven in a pagan spirit, with a narrow-minded selfishness that cares nothing for others, and is simply an extension to the future life of the grabbing spirit fostered by the Kingdom of Evil. The desire for heaven gets Christian dignity and quality only when it arises on the basis of that solidaristic state of mind which is cultivated by the social gospel.[78]

The most unattractive element Rauschenbusch saw in the orthodox concept of eternal life was the immediate fixity of the two states. Instead of this concept, he offered the idea of an ascending scale toward God reaching from the lowest to the highest in which each person would have one's place according to one's own spiritual growth that he or she had obtained in earthly life. This would allow for spiritual growth in the future life that would come by continued love and service. He saw no idleness in the future life, but believed that those who had advanced further in holy experience here would labor in helping others who had not advanced as far in their spiritual growth.[79] "Is this training to go for nothing in heaven, or is this present life the real preparation for the kind of life we are to live there, and the basis for promotion and growth?"[80]

E. Stanley Jones gave a similar emphasis on eternal growth when he said,

> I believe that we begin in heaven where we leave off here. This means that rewards in heaven are not arbitrarily given for faithful service to God. The reward is in the quality of being we take with us. We will start in heaven with the capacity for the enjoyment of God we have developed here. The greater the capacity we take with us, the greater the enjoyment of God, hence the greater the reward. We won't even know he has a greater reward—only God and he will know that. Hence there can be no asking for bonuses or jostling for rewards. There will be no first seats or peanut galleries; everyone will take from the Infinite what his capacity for taking will allow. Everyone's cup will be full, but some cups will be larger. They made them so through the years.[81]

Rauschenbusch would not have called himself a Universalist, but his view of eschatology certainly seems to depict a concept of universal salvation. In his view of an ascending scale toward God, a person would be as far from God and be in as much darkness and narrowness as she deserved by her life on earth, but there would always be the possibility of growth. This, he felt, would satisfy our sense of justice better and would summon men and women to more self-discipline than the view that when a person is "saved," he is "saved" completely and escapes all future consequences. A person might have been "saved" personally and yet may have been responsible for the retardation of many others in society. He could, therefore, Rauschenbusch conjectured, have the responsibility of leading these to the source of love and life and in doing so would continue to grow in his own spiritual insight.[82]

In his ascending scale of being, Rauschenbusch pictured no one so high that he could not still be drawn closer to God and no one so low that he could be beyond God's love. God was envisioned as one who would always be teaching and saving all men and women. Rauschenbusch believed that no Christian could rejoice in the idea of an eternal hell, and that this doctrine could not be tolerable when one conceived of God as a Father dealing with his children.

Punishment could no longer be viewed as wholly without end or change but should be seen as educational and redemptive.[83] He felt that something would die in heaven if God allowed a minority to remain in a permanent hell. If anyone chose to remain in darkness, Rauschenbusch asserted that there would be a Christian invasion of hell itself: "All the most Christian souls in heaven would get down there and share the life of the wicked, in the high hope that after all some scintilla of heavenly fire was still smoldering and could be fanned into life. And they would be headed by Him who could not stand it to think of ninety-nine saved and one caught among the thorns."[84]

Rauschenbusch affirmed his faith in the belief in eternal life[85] but sought to bring men and women to the realization that this view did not negate the importance of Christian action in this world. He felt that all people were to labor here in the Kingdom of God so that God's will could be done on earth as it was in heaven, and the more one absorbed the laws of the Kingdom into his or her character here, the greater would be one's participation in the future life.[86] However, he did feel that there were only a few things that one could claim with any assurance about the concept of eternal life.

> These are: that the love of God will go out forever to his children, and especially to the neediest, drawing them to him and, where necessary, saving them; that personality energized by God is ever growing; that the law of love and solidarity will be even more effective in heaven than on earth; and that salvation, growth and solidarity are conditioned on interchange of service.[87]

Although Rauschenbusch has been accused of not having a substantial concept of personal salvation, it appears that this is not a valid criticism. His concept of the sacredness of every human personality called for personal redemption, but with this experience he always asserted that men and women had to realize their solidaristic involvement with humanity. He felt that an individual's personal religious experience should not be reduced to subjective mysticism, nor should it be enervated by another-worldly asceticism. His view of eternal life revealed a concept of universal salvation that depicted an ascending scale of being in which growth was possible and continuous. The concept of eternal life, Rauschenbusch declared, was not to minimize the importance of this life; for it was here that a person's degree of participation in the future life was determined. Those who had experienced God personally were "saved" from the Kingdom of Evil and were now to be engaged actively in the Kingdom of God.

Notes

1. Shailer Mathews, "The Book of the Month," *The Biblical World* 41 (February 1913): 138.

2. WR, "Ideals of Social Reformers," *American Journal of Sociology* 2 (September 1896): 210.

3. WR, *The Social Principles of Jesus* (New York: Association Press, 1917) 10.

4. Ibid., 31.

5. Ibid., 8–9.

6. Ibid., 4.

7. In William A. Mueller, "The Life, Work and Gospel of Walter Rauschenbusch," *Religion in Life* 15 (Autumn 1946): 538.

8. WR, *The Social Principles of Jesus*, 12.

9. Ibid., 13.

10. Ibid., 9.

11. Ibid., 10.

12. Ibid., 14.

13. A. T. Robertson, *The New Citizenship* (New York: Fleming H. Revell Company, 1919) 149.

14. Tony Campolo, "A Response by an Evangelical," in WR, *Christianity and the Social Crisis for the 21st Century* (New York: HarperOne, 2007) 78.

15. Paul Brandeis Raushenbush, "Foreword," in WR, *Christianity and the Social Crisis for the 21st Century*, xv, referring to a blog entry by Warren.

16. C. Douglas Weaver, *In Search of the New Testament Church: The Baptist Story* (Macon GA: Mercer University Press, 2008) 125.

17. WR, *The Social Principles of Jesus*, 81.

18. WR, "Revelation: An Exposition," *Biblical World* 10 (August 1897): 102.

19. WR, *Christianizing the Social Order* (New York: Macmillan Company, 1912) 464.

20. WR, *The Righteousness of the Kingdom*, ed. Max L. Stackhouse (Nashville: Abingdon Press, 1968) 99.

21. WR, *Christianity and the Social Crisis* (New York: Macmillan Company, 1907) 367.

22. WR, *A Theology for the Social Gospel* (New York: Macmillan Company, 1917) 95.

23. Mueller, "The Life, Work and Gospel of Walter Rauschenbusch."

24. WR, *Christianizing the Social Order*, 104.

25. Dores R. Sharpe, *Walter Rauschenbusch* (New York: Macmillan Company, 1912) 104.

26. WR, *Christianity and the Social Crisis*, 351.

27. Ibid., 366.

28. Ibid., 366–67, 351, 412. See also WR, *The Social Principles of Jesus*, 5, 81, 89, 158–59; *Christianizing the Social Order*, 103–104, 460–62; *A Theology for the Social Gospel*, 95ff.

29. WR, *Christianizing the Social Order*, 460.

30. *The Rochester Theological Seminary Record*, November 1918, p. 43.

31. Harlan Beckley, *Passion for Justice: Retrieving the Legacies of Walter Rauschenbusch, John A. Ryan, and Reinhold Niebuhr* (Louisville: Westminster/John Knox, 1992) 81. (See in particular WR, *Christianizing the Social Order*, 458ff., and *Christianity and the Social Crisis*, 411ff.)

32. WR, "Revelation: An Exposition," 95.

33. Ibid., 101.

34. WR, "Influence of Historical Studies on Theology," *American Journal of Theology* 11 (January 1907): 127.

35. WR, "Revelation: An Exposition," 97.

36. WR, "The Rights of the Children in the Community," *Religious Education* 10 (June 1915): 224–25.

37. WR, *Christianizing the Social Order*, 40.

38. WR, *A Theology for the Social Gospel*, 176.

39. Ibid.

40. Ibid., 152–53.

41. WR, "Why I Am a Baptist," *A Baptist Treasury*, ed. Sydnor L. Stealey (New York: Thomas Y. Crowell Company, 1958) 169.

42. Ibid., 169.

43. Ibid., 166.

44. *The Rochester Theological Seminary Record*, 39.

45. Sharpe, *Walter Rauschenbusch*, 393.

46. Ibid., 395. Sharpe quoting Rauschenbusch's "Social Motives in Evangelism," unpublished.

47. Ibid., 84–85.

48. Donald B. Meyer, *The Protestant Search for Political Realism, 1919–1941* (Berkeley: University of California Press, 1960) 133.

49. *The Rochester Theological Seminary Record*, 39.

50. Sharpe, *Walter Rauschenbusch*, 436.

51. *The Rochester Theological Seminary Record*, 34–35.

52. WR, *A Theology for the Social Gospel*, 105.

53. Richard Rorty, "Buds That Never Opened," in WR, *Christianity and the Social Crisis in the 21st Century*, 348–49.

53. Walter Rauschenbusch, "A Thanksgiving Day Homily," 1898, quoted in Darlene Ann Peitz, *Solidarity as Hermeneutic: A Revisionist Reading of the Theology of Walter Rauschenbusch* (New York: Peter Lang Publishing, Inc., 1992) v.

54. Ibid., 98.

55. Ibid., 99.

56. Ibid., 101–102.

57. Ibid.

58. J. S. Whale, *Christian Doctrine* (Glasgow: Fontana Books, 1958) 119–20.

59. WR, *Unto Me* (New York: Pilgrim Press, 1912) 18.

60. WR, *Christianizing the Social Order*, 465.

61. WR, *A Theology for the Social Gospel*, 96–97.

62. Ibid., 96.

63. Ibid., 108.

64. Ibid., 104.

65. Ibid.

66. Ibid., 155.

67. Ibid., 104.

68. Ibid., 106.

69. Ibid., 107.

70. Ibid., 108.

71. WR, *Christianity and the Social Crisis*, 164–65.

72. Ibid., 174.

73. Ibid., 173.

74. Ibid., 175.

75. WR, *A Theology for the Social Gospel*, 228–29.

76. WR, *Christianity and the Social Crisis*, 107.

77. Ibid., 162.

78. WR, *A Theology for the Social Gospel*, 229–30.

79. Ibid., 232–26.

80. Ibid., 236.

81. E. Stanley Jones, *Growing Spiritually* (New York: Abingdon Press, 1953) 363.

82. WR, *A Theology for the Social Gospel*, 235–38.

83. Ibid., 215.

84. Ibid., 234. For some who have written about this theme, see Rob Bell, *Love Wins* (New York: HarperOne, 2010); William Barclay, *A Spiritual Autobiography* (Grand Rapids MI: William B. Eerdmans, 1975) 60ff.; Nels F. S. Ferré, *The Christian Understanding of God* (New York: Harper & Brothers, 1951) 229ff.; Molly T. Marshall, *No Salvation Outside the Church: A Critical Inquiry* (Lampeter, Wales: Edwin Press, Ltd., 1993) 231ff.; and Marshall, *Trinitarian Soundings* (Shawnee KS: Central Baptist Theological Seminary, 2011) 45f.; Dale Moody, *The Word of Truth* (Grand Rapids MI: William B. Eerdmans Publishing Co., 1981) 496f.; Jurgen Moltmann, *The Coming of God* (Minneapolis: Fortress Press, 1996) 252–54; William Powell Tuck, *Journey to the Undiscovered Country: What's Beyond Death?* (Gonzalez FL: Energion Publications, 2012) 52ff.; William H. Willimon, *Who Will Be Saved?* (Nashville: Abingdon Press, 2008); N. T. Wright, *Surprised by Hope: Rethinking Heaven, the Resurrection and the Mission of the Church* (New York: HarperOne, 2008) 104–108, 114–17,148–51.

85. Benson Y. Landis (comp.), *A Rauschenbusch Reader* (New York: Harper and Brothers, 1957) 149.

86. WR, *A Theology for the Social Gospel*, 238–39.

87. Ibid., 238.

Chapter 6

The Concept of Social Redemption

Rauschenbusch's doctrine of soteriology involved not only a concept of personal redemption but also a concept of social redemption. This chapter will examine the following aspects of his concept of social redemption: the social implications of salvation; the atonement and racial solidarity; the redemption of the super-personal entities; and the church as the social factor in redemption.

The Social Implications of Salvation

One of the basic presuppositions underlying Rauschenbusch's whole theology, and one that he amplified in all his writings, was that humanity's relationship to God could not be reduced merely to an atomistic individualism, but that men and women were solidaristically involved with all of humanity. People were seen as being involved with the corporate life of humanity, and therefore the Christian could never be an antinomian. No person could claim to have "faith" in God and repudiate the moral law. Religion and ethics were to be viewed as inseparable. "Rauschenbusch's concept of social salvation," Christopher Evans declares, "was inseparable from his major contribution to American theology: his reinterpretation of the Christian doctrine of the kingdom of God."[1] In writing *The Righteousness of the Kingdom* (which he penned before his other well-received books and which was not published until 1968, long after his death), Rauschenbusch reveals that he believed that the teachings of Jesus were revolutionary, especially as they related to the Kingdom of God on earth and the sanctification of this life. He expounded that view this way:

> It [the Kingdom of God] includes a twofold aim: the regeneration of every individual to divine sonship and eternal life, and the victory of the spirit of Christ over the spirit of this world in every form of human society and a corresponding alteration in all the institutions formed in human society. These two are simultaneous aims. Every success in the one is a means for a new success in the other.[2]

Rauschenbusch said that his main purpose in writing *A Theology for the Social Gospel* was to show that the social gospel was a vital part of the Christian concept of sin and salvation and that any theology that failed to give a significant place to the social factors and processes in sin and salvation would be incomplete, unreal, and misleading.[3] He insisted that one of the rudiments of the Christian faith was that love to God must have its counterpoise in love for others: "Men tell us that religion ought to have an ethical outcome and that love to God is inseparable from love to men. They say it as if that were a new discovery. It ought to be a truism by this time."[4] He reiterated this point by saying,

> No man is a follower of Jesus in the full sense who has not through him entered into the same life with God. But on the other hand no man shares his life with God whose religion does not flow out, naturally and without effort, into all relations of his life and reconstructs everything that it touches. Whoever uncouples the religious and the social life has not understood Jesus.[5]

The Christian's aim, Rauschenbusch believed, was not to pass through an evil world in safety, leaving the world's evil unshaken; rather, it was to seek a moral and religious transformation of humanity in all of its social relations.[6] Christianity was to be an invasion of one's whole life or none of it. Rauschenbusch would be in agreement with the statement that "God is not the benign manager of a hotel of heaven, the final resort for the respectable who practice private purity. He is a living God who requires evenhandedness and integrity, justice and mercy."[7] "We love and serve God," Rauschenbusch stated, "when we love and serve our fellows, whom he loves and in whom he lives."[8] Because of his concept of an altruistic Christianity, Rauschenbusch put more emphasis on the immanence of God than on transcendence. He believed that God was transcendent, but he felt that any view of Christianity that overemphasized the transcendence of God made God remote, therefore minimizing the relationship of salvation to this world and causing neglect in social reconstruction.

Rauschenbusch interpreted the nature of sin as being not simply a private matter between a person and God but as a solidaristic concept that unified humanity in a common involvement in the Kingdom of evil. This called individuals to an awareness of their personal responsibility for the common sin of humanity in which all share and to which all people contribute. The doctrine of original sin was also treated as a social concept. He saw sin as being transmitted along the line of social tradition and assimilation rather than merely along biological lines. The belief in a satanic kingdom was also reinterpreted to denote a solidaristic concept of evil so that humanity would continue to be concerned only with transient individualistic sins. Rauschenbusch's doctrine of sin was expanded to include the concept of collective and social sins, and thus he also called for an expansion in the scope of salvation. "If evil is socialized," he insisted, "salvation must be socialized."[9]

Rauschenbusch's concept of salvation, therefore, seems to be a natural theological outworking of his doctrine of sin. His social gospel had called for an expansion in the scope of sin, and his concept of salvation was also expanded to include social redemption. "There are two great entities in human life,—the human soul and the human race,—and religion is to save both."[10] Salvation was conceived as being concerned not only with a reformation within individual lives but also with a reformation of social forces and entities. Redemption would not be complete until there was a regenerated society as well as regenerated individuals. The Kingdom of God was envisioned as the organism through which social redemption would be actualized in this world.

> The Kingdom of God is still a collective conception, involving the whole social life of man. It is not a matter of saving the social organism. It is not a matter of getting individuals to heaven, but of

transforming the life on earth into the harmony of heaven . . . . But Jesus never fell in the fundamental heresy of later theology; he never viewed the human individual apart from human society; he never forgot the gregarious nature of man. His first appeal was to his nation.[11]

Each individual personality was of eternal value for its own sake, but one's religious individuality always needed to be interpreted as a part of humankind and to be seen in terms of social solidarity. Christianizing the social order in Rauschenbusch's opinion was, therefore, not like repairing a clock in which one or two parts might be broken and repaired individually. Rather, it was thought to be like the restoration of diseased or wasted tissues that put every organ and cell in the body under heavy taxation.[12] "The conception of race sin and race salvation become comprehensible once more to those who have made the idea of social solidarity in good and evil a part of their thought."[13] The emphasis that Rauschenbusch put on the necessity of a solidaristic comprehension of sin and salvation can be seen in the following statement:

> The definition of sin as selfishness gets its reality and nipping force only when we see humanity as a great solidarity and God indwelling in it. In the same way the terms and definitions of salvation get more realistic significance and ethical reach when we see the internal crises of the individual in connection with the social forces that play upon him or go out from him. The form which the process of redemption takes in a given personality will be determined by the historical and social spiritual environment of the man. At any rate any religious experience in which our fellow-men have no part or thought, does not seem to be a distinctively Christian experience.[14]

Rauschenbusch's concept of social redemption was harshly criticized by many conservative voices in his day. One of the most vocal of these was a premillennial preacher, I. M. Haldeman, who was pastor of the First Baptist Church in New York City. He wrote in 1911 his version of the purpose of the coming of Christ as a rebuke to Rauschenbusch's concept of collective salvation.

> It was not because society was corrupt and needed bettering that he [Jesus] came. It was not because he would ameliorate society and save it that he spoke his parables and wrought his deeds, but because the fullness of time had come to offer to the chosen people the kingdom promised to their fathers. Whether society were good or bad did not enter into the matter. He was on time in obedience to the eternal counsels and to fulfill the Word of God. . . . He turns from society altogether, makes no provision to save it, and occupies himself thenceforward with warning the individual soul of its need of salvation.[15]

To premillennialism thinkers like Haldeman, Christianity was to have nothing to do with this world. The world was interpreted as being under the control of sin and could not be redeemed, and the only hope for men and women was to escape from this world. The Christian church was not to attempt to correct society or its problems but was to concern itself only with pointing to the "blood-stained substitute," and to a remote Lord who would one day return to take his followers out of this world. The premillennial concept of Christianity as presented by Haldeman was in complete antitheses to Rauschenbusch's view of Christianity. Rauschenbusch urged his readers to compare Haldeman's criticism of his book, *Christianity and the Social Crisis*, side by side with the book itself and then choose between the two types of Christianity presented. Speaking of Haldeman's pamphlet, Rauschenbusch said, "It is an emphatic condemnation of my position and uncompromising statement of the apocalyptic scheme and spirit in all of its dogmatic assurance and artificiality."[16]

George Marsden in his book, *Fundamentalism and American Culture*, notes that conservative evangelicals thought that the threat from the social gospel theology challenged traditional Christian belief. "The Social Gospel presented, or was thought to be presented," Marsden alleges, "as equivalent to the Gospel itself."[17] The evangelicals who had warned that the social gospel interests would inevitably undermine concern for right belief and salvation of souls, he continues, believed that they now had confirmation for their claims.[18]

Rauschenbusch had little patience with any view of Christianity that did not see it as a transforming force in the present world. To deny the social implications of salvation was to him a complete misunderstanding of the very purpose of salvation itself. Salvation was concerned with both the personality of individuals and the collective personality of humanity. Therefore, Christianity was to offer to the individual person victory over sin and death, and to humanity it was to offer a perfect social life with justice, equality, and love.[19] In Rauschenbusch's opinion, salvation could never be completely understood until one realized its social implications. He asserted that although Jesus was not a social reformer in the modern-day sense, he directed his message to people in a way that was profoundly social. "Jesus nourished within his own soul," Rauschenbusch argued, "the ideal of a common life so radically different from the present that it involved a reversal of values, a revolutionary displacement of existing relations."[20] Salvation was always to be interpreted in light of the solidaristic comprehension furnished by the social gospel. "A full salvation demands a Christian social order which will serve as the spiritual environment of the individual."[21]

The Atonement and Racial Solidarity

Nowhere is Rauschenbusch's concept of racial solidarity more clearly seen than in his concept of the atonement. He realized that to most Christian minds, the doctrine of the atonement was the marrow of theology, and therefore he sought to examine this doctrine in light of the social gospel's concept of solidarity. Many questions, he felt, were raised by the death of Christ, and many of the answers that had been given were inadequate and had not taken into account the social solidarity of mankind.

> As Christian men we believe that the death of our Lord concerns us all. Our sins caused it. He bore the sin of the world. In turn his death was somehow for our good. Our spiritual situation is fundamentally changed in consequence of it. But how? How did he bear our sins? How did his death affect God? How did it affect us?[22]

In a lecture that Rauschenbusch gave in the fall of 1885 at Rochester Seminary on "The Bushnellian Theory of the Atonement," he questioned the "ransom" or "substitutionary" views of the atonement that depicted the death of Jesus as a "payment" for the sins of humanity. He argued instead for a "moral influence" view of the atonement, based on Horace Bushnell's interpretation, which did not see Jesus' death as an appeasement for the wrath of an angry God against sinful humanity but instead as a way of reconciliation for sinful humanity to a loving God. Drawing on the parable of the Prodigal Son, he believed that human sin saddened the heart of God because it caused an absence from God's presence, but God welcomed the sinners back by divine love. "If they do not come," he continued, "they will have to bear the terrible consequence of their refusal."[23]

Rauschenbusch felt that the old theological interpretation that Jesus bore our sins by imputation was incorrect. Jesus did not bear humanity's sin by imputation, because guilt and merit, Rauschenbusch stated, are personal and cannot be transferred from one person to another. In his opinion, imputation was merely a legal device to enable the law to hold another person responsible for a crime committed by someone else. He felt that this interpretation pictured humanity as a great mass of individuals who transferred their debts individually to Christ.[24] An ethical conception of salvation in his opinion was always superior to a forensic view, because the language of the courtroom was likely to leave out one of the most important aspects of God's character—God's love. "But expressions borrowed from family life are better than legal expressions, because in the family justice and love are blended, and modify each other."[25]

Neither did Rauschenbusch envision Jesus as bearing humanity's sins by mere sympathy. He felt that Jesus was bound up with the life of humanity by actual experience: "The bar to a true understanding of the atonement has been our individualism. The solution of the problem lies in the recognition of solidarity."[26] Rauschenbusch's concept of sin has revealed his emphasis on the organized forces and institutions of evil that he saw culminated in the Kingdom of Evil. Jesus lived in the midst of the Kingdom of Evil, Rauschenbusch noted, and it was this public and organized evil that killed him and not merely the personal transgression of individual men who were living then. These collective sins, many of which Rauschenbusch viewed as still existing, emerged on Jesus and killed him.[27] He wrote, "Jesus did not in any real sense bear the sin of some ancient Briton who beat up his wife in BC 56, or of some mountaineer in Tennessee who got drunk in AD 1917. But he did in a very real sense bear the weight of the public sins of organized society, and they in turn are causally connected with all private sins."[28]

Rauschenbusch enumerated six sins, all of a public nature, that he felt combined to bring about the death of Jesus: religious bigotry, as embodied at that time in the intellectual expounders and devotees of Judaism; the combination of graft and political power of the ruling class of the Jews; the corruption of justice in both the Roman and the Jewish ecclesiastical courts; mob spirit and mob action that resulted in the intoxication of the social spirit; militarism as seen in the military forces of the Roman Empire; and class contempt that was revealed in the fact that only members of the lowest classes suffered the fate of crucifixion. Religious bigotry, the combination of graft and political power, the corruption of justice, the mob spirit, militarism, and class contempt were the sins that Jesus bore in a very real sense, Rauschenbusch declared, although he had not contributed to them as the rest of humanity had. The personal sins of men and women had contributed to the existence of these public sins, and therefore Jesus came into collision with the totality of evil. These were the social sins of all humankind; and all who have ever lived have contributed to them, and all who have ever lived have suffered under them.[29]

Rauschenbusch believed that his view of the solidaristic interpretation of the death of Jesus was the very manner in which Jesus had regarded his own death. Rauschenbusch pointed to the parable of the vineyard, which he felt Jesus used to depict the historical, social, and solidaristic interpretation of his own death. Jesus had pointed to the history of Israel as a continuous struggle with the exploiters of religion on one side and God's prophets on the other, and then he pictured his death as being the culmination of the prophetic succession. Jesus warned his own generation that they were about to repeat the same sin that he had pointed to in the parable of the vineyard if they persecuted the new prophets he was going to send out. Rauschenbusch interpreted Jesus' meaning to declare that by repeating the sins of the past, one becomes involved in the guilt of the past.³⁰ Men and women then become linked in a solidarity of evil and guilt. "In so far then as we, by our conscious actions or our passive consent, have repeated the sins which killed Jesus, we have made ourselves guilty of his death."³¹

The following summary statement reveals the manner in which Rauschenbusch believed Jesus bore the sins of the world.

> Along two lines we have replied to the question how the sins of the world were borne by Jesus: First, the realistic forces which killed Jesus were not accidental and personal causes of his death, but were the reaction of the totality of racial sin against him; and second, the guilt of those who did it spreads to all who reaffirm the acts which killed him. The key to the problem is contained in the realization of solidarity.³²

In attempting to understand how the death of Jesus affected God and changed the relation of humanity toward him, Rauschenbusch believed that the first step was to see the death of Jesus as an integral part of his life. He regarded the spiritual and redemptive value of the death of Jesus not in the quantity of his mental or physical suffering but in his willingness to take upon himself the highest and hardest part of his life's work. The whole life of Jesus had been given in love and service, and his death had the same significance. His death was the culmination of his life's work and was its most luminous moment. For in his death was revealed the most dramatic expression of his personality and the most consistent assertion of the purpose and law for which he had lived.³³

Rauschenbusch observed that any attempt to answer how the death of Jesus affected God would be inadequate. In his opinion, the only sure guide in speaking of God was the mind of Jesus, which was to be humanity's logic and metaphysics. Rauschenbusch believed, though, that if "Christ was the Divine Logos," then the death of Jesus must have been a great experience for God himself. "If the principle of forgiving love had not been in the heart of God before, this experience would fix it there."³⁴

Rauschenbusch also believed that Jesus changed the relationship between God and humanity. While humanity continues to live in the Kingdom of Evil, people are not in spiritual fellowship with God and God is forced to oppose individuals instead of loving and helping them, which God really desires to do. Christ was envisioned by Rauschenbusch to be the first one to live fully within the consciousness of God, and he drew others into the realization of God so that they could also love God freely and live within his will. Christ was the initiator of the beginning of the Kingdom of God within the race, and his position was unique; but his "sin" was not to be unique but to be "the first born among many brethren." Christ opened the way for man and God to have a cooperative unity of will and to be able to enter into a spiritual solidarity.[35]

In this process of reconciliation, Rauschenbusch reasoned that the death of Jesus had no place apart from his life. The death of Jesus, he believed, had to be taken in connection with the purpose of his whole life and seen as a climax to his prophetic career. His death did, however, have an essential place in establishing solidarity and reconciliation between God and humanity. Rauschenbusch saw it as the supreme act of opposition to sin, and of complete obedience to God.[36] He felt that this conception could be utilized by the social gospel.

> This conception is free from the artificial and immoral elements inherent in all forensic and governmental interpretations of the atonement. It begins with the solidarity between God and Christ, and proceeds to the solidarity between God and mankind. It deals with social and religious realities. It connects the idea of reconciliation and the idea of the Kingdom of God. It does not dispense with the moral effort of men and the moral renewal of social life but absolutely demands both.[37]

Rauschenbusch believed that the atonement affected humanity in at least three ways. He saw it first as the conclusive demonstration of the power of sin in humanity. He felt that no one could contemplate the great power of the social and racial sins that had converged on Jesus without having a deep sense of the enormous power of evil in the world and of the great task before the Kingdom of God. "The cross forever puts a question mark alongside of any easy treatment of sin," he said.[38]

In the second place, he saw the death of Christ as the supreme revelation of love. Jesus had put love in the center of all his teachings, and his life had been an exemplification of all that he had taught, and his death had underscored all that he had said on love. By his death, Jesus furnished the chief guarantee for the love of God and the chief incentive for self-sacrificing love among humanity. The love of God as revealed in the atonement also enables humanity to see that salvation is a gift and cannot be earned. The cross continues to stand as the monumental fact telling all people of God's grace and inviting them to repentance and humility.[39]

> Thus the death of Christ was the conclusive and effective expression of the love of Jesus Christ for God and man, and his complete devotion to the Kingdom of God. The more his personality was understood to be the full and complete expression of the character of God, the more did his death become the assurance and guarantee that God loves us, forgives us, and is willing to do all things to save us.[40]

Third, Rauschenbusch believed that the death of Christ reinforced prophetic religion. The priest in his opinion was the religious professional, while the prophet represented one who had had a personal experience with God that he wanted to share with all people. His religious experience caused him to have quickening of social consciousness and to speak out for justice, righteousness, and compassion. The prophets, Rauschenbusch felt, were usually regarded as heretics, free thinkers, enemies of religion, or atheists. Their opposition to social injustice usually aroused antagonism from those who profited by it. The death of Jesus was considered the clearest and most conspicuous instance of prophetic suffering, and those who had to bear prophetic suffering, he felt, could receive comfort from the fact that they were carrying on what Jesus had done. The cross of Christ strengthened the power of prophetic religion, and the social gospel was the continuation of the voice of prophecy in the modern world.[41]

Evans notes that H. Richard Niebuhr had criticized the liberal theology of some of Rauschenbusch's components for lacking an emphasis on divine judgment and human suffering. Evans says that Rauschenbusch's sermons had a special emphasis on vicarious suffering, and the themes of divine judgment and human suffering "were central to his theological imperative to work for the kingdom of God."[42] Niebuhr had observed that in Rauschenbusch's thought, unlike some of the other social gospel proclaimers, "the reign of Christ required conversion and the coming kingdom was crisis, judgment as well as promise." Continuing, he said, "Though his theory of the relation of God and man often seemed liberal he continued to speak the language of the prophets and St. Paul."[43]

Rauschenbusch was aware that social redemption would not come easily. "The coming of the Kingdom of God will not be by peaceful development only but by conflict with the Kingdom of Evil. We should estimate the power of sin too lightly if we forecast a smooth road."[44] In his book, *The Social Principles of Jesus*, Rauschenbusch has a chapter titled "The Cross as a Social Principle." He reminds his readers that pain and suffering was often a product for those striving to bring about social justice. Like the vicarious suffering of Jesus, the followers of Jesus often discovered that suffering accompanied those who opposed the Kingdom of Evil as they labored for the Kingdom of God.[45] "Jesus himself linked his own suffering and rejection with the fate of the prophets who were before him," Rauschenbusch observed, "and with the fate of the disciples who would come after him. He saw a red line running through history, and his own life and death were part of it."[46]

Rauschenbusch had once prayed, "May thy cross never be to us a device of theology, but make it a power to awaken in us a living passion for thee and thy service."[47] The cross had not been a mere device of theology to him, but in it he had seen the revelation of God's eternal love, and the great power of sin. Rauschenbusch saw the solution to the problem of the atonement in the recognition of racial solidarity. The concept of solidarity was his decisive point of argument.

The Redemption of the Super-personal Entities

In considering Rauschenbusch's doctrine of sin, it was seen that he believed that the responsibility for sin lay not only on the individual man but also on forces that he called super-personal entities. These super-personal forces were enumerated as complex spiritual entities that were beyond the individual.[48] The idea, which he derived from Royce, pictured "in the human world two profoundly different grades, or levels, of mental beings,—namely, the beings that we usually call human individuals, and the beings that we call communities."[49] The super-personal entities were seen as powerful forces of evil, and he noted that unless they were adequately taken into consideration by theology, the concepts of sin and salvation would be unrelated to some of the most important work of redemption.[50]

The super-personal forces were seen as exerting a powerful authority over their members and rendering a strong influence over the general social life of humanity. They were seen as the most powerful ethical forces in the communities.[51] These forces, such as political parties, business organizations, churches, social groups, and other combinations of individuals, could become evil, and when these super-personal entities became corrupted they blocked the way of redemption and were considered by Rauschenbusch in the same light as earlier Christian minds had conceived of demonic personalities.[52] Like the individual person, these super-personal forces were seen as needing regeneration. "The salvation of the composite personalities, like that of individuals, consists in coming under the law of Christ."[53] David True, after his extensive study of Rauschenbusch's works, concludes, "For Rauschenbusch, Christianity was about the transformation of all of life. God's intended reign is comprehensive. Loyalty to God calls for all things, including politics, to be transformed so that they serve God's purposes."[54]

Rauschenbusch believed that four sections of the American social order had already been Christianized: the family, the organized religious life, the institutions of education, and the political organization of the nation.[55] This Christianization of a large segment of the social order, he felt, meant that the larger part of the work of social redemption had been accomplished.⁵⁶ One would certainly not agree with this statement today, and it is felt that if Rauschenbusch were living now, it is also unlikely that he would make the same judgment. He longed for the ultimate redemption of the social order, and sometimes his realistic view of the sinful nature of humanity was not completely balanced by the optimism that he envisioned in the Christianization of the social order itself. Ross Douthat, in his book, *Bad Religion: How We Became a Religion of Heretics*, asserts that Rauschenbusch downplayed original sin and held to an overoptimistic view of the latent perfectability of human nature. He further contends that Rauschenbusch subordinated faith to Social Darwinism, divinized progress, and treated secular history as the only dispositive revelation of God's purpose on earth.⁵⁷ Although this may have been true of some social gospel "preachers," it is not a valid criticism of Rauschenbusch. Frederick Sontag and John Roth point in particular to Rauschenbusch's linking the labor movement with the push toward the Christian socialism he envisioned. "The moral to be learned is this: *Christianity should risk social action*," they aver, "*but to link Christianity too simplistically with any one economic program is to encourage religious obsolescence when change eludes our control and takes unintended forms.*"⁵⁸

Rauschenbusch, however, did not hold to a naïve optimism of inevitable progress for the Christianization of society. He realized that the advance of the Kingdom of God could come only by conflict with powerful evil forces. He warned that "any effort at social regeneration is dogged by perpetual relapses and doomed forever to fall short of its goal."⁵⁹ His doctrine of sin reveals clearly the struggle that he saw confronting the advance of the Kingdom of God. "We should estimate the power of sin too lightly if we forecast a smooth road."⁶⁰ Affirming an optimistic view of the future, nevertheless, Rauschenbusch was aware that the social struggle for righteousness would be difficult.

> We ask for no Utopian delusion. We know well that there is no perfection for man in this life: there is only growth toward perfection. In personal religion we look with seasoned suspicion at any one who claims to be holy and perfect, yet we always tell men to

become holy and seek perfection. We make it a duty to seek what is unattainable. We have the same paradox in the perfection of society. We shall never have a perfect social life, yet we must seek it with faith.... At best there is always but an approximation to a perfect social order. The kingdom of God is always but coming.[61]

He noted that continents were strewn with the ruins of dead nations that had felt that their civilization would never end. "History," he said, "laughs at the optimistic illusion that 'nothing can stand in the way of human progress.'"[62] Ernest Johnson affirms Rauschenbusch's concern about the naïve optimism that would assume an easy victory against the forces of evil: "Rauschenbusch, Gladden, Strong and Taylor—to mention only a few—would have difficulty in recognizing themselves in current deliverances against what is alleged to be the easy, romantic optimism of the social gospel!"[63] "Those who accuse Rauschenbusch of a ready identification of contemporary finite achievements with the absolute victory of the Kingdom did not read him carefully," Rosemary Ruether observed. "Rauschenbusch's vision is not one of finalizing any finite achievement, but rather one of continuous growth and aspiration, never perfected in history yet communing with that ultimate Kingdom in each momentary and partial victory."[64] In Rauschenbusch's opinion, a decisive point had been reached in the history of Western civilization. And in contemplation of the future of this civilization he asked, "Will some Gibbon of Mongol race sit by the shore of the Pacific in the year AD 3000 and write on the 'Decline and Fall of the Christian Empire'?"[65] Some like Stanley Hauerwas have accused Rauschenbusch of reducing the Kingdom of God to a democratic America.[66] But this is a misreading of Rauschenbusch's view. Rauschenbusch held to no utopian optimism about the Christian nations. He felt that there had to be either a revival of social religion or a great deluge. "It rests upon us to decide if a new era is to dawn in the transformation of the world into the kingdom of God," he wrote, "or if Western civilization is to descend to the graveyard of dead civilizations and God will have to try once more."[67]

In an unpublished ordination sermon, "The Sower," delivered at Minneapolis, Minnesota, on April 25, 1909, Rauschenbusch revealed in a vivid fashion that he held to no naïve optimism concerning the work of the Christian ministry.

> It is an absolute certainty that much of his work [a Christian minister's work] will be spoiled for him. With all the earnestness of his soul he sends a thought out to the people; he moves a young soul, but a frivolous friend on the way home undoes it all. He seeks to brace a young man to keep his sensual appetites under control, but a great commercial corporation subsidizes saloons all along our streets to decoy the young fellow and turn his soul into dividends for the brewing and distilling companies. He preaches to men on the life of brotherly helpfulness and self-sacrifice as Jesus wants it, and all the facts of our business life contradict and tell a man to look out for himself, for nobody else will look out for him.
>
> The minister's work is destined to partial failure. In some ways the higher and nobler it is, the greater will be the percentage of failure. Let every minister face this fact. Jesus warned men to consider the risk if they followed him and not to build a house if they had not the wherewithal to finish it or to follow him if they would not share his homelessness.[68]

Rauschenbusch saw that a vast source of the evil in the present social order emanated out of our nation's business life. The economic segment of our social order was the most in need of Christian redemption. "Business life is the unregenerate section of our social order."[69] Its only hope of redemption was to come under the law of Christ. "It is the function of religion to teach society to value human life more than property," Rauschenbusch asserted, "and to value property only in so far as it forms the material basis for higher development of human life."[70] He noted that there were two principles contending for future control in the area of industrial and commercial organization. These two organizations were the capitalistic and the cooperative. He believed that the capitalistic principle of organization was under the law of Mammon because its chief emphasis was on profit and it consequently resulted in the application of exploiting and oppressive methods. It had strengthened the autocratic principle and had left a materialistic spirit on the civilization of humanity.

But he believed that cooperative organizations were founded on the principle of the satisfaction of human wants and not primarily for profit motives, and therefore their aim is to distribute ownership, control, and economic benefits to a large number of cooperators. For this reason, he thought the cooperatives were under the law of Christ and the capitalistic organization was not.[71] He argued strongly against the upperclass minds who throughout history had lived off peasants and their tenants to pay for their leisure. He spoke out against monopoly profits and the private control of investments and called for democratization of power and a form of socialism.[72] However, Martin Marty wonders why anyone ever considered the social gospel proponents radical. He saw them as more timid in their call for social reform than far-reaching in their programmatic suggestions.[73] In contrast to this perspective, Christopher Evans quotes Martin Luther King, Jr., saying that "what set the social gospel apart was the way that its understanding of the social dimension of human experience was used to rethink the categories of Christian Theology." Continuing, he is bold to declare, "For many, this enterprise of theological reformation was nothing short of a second Reformation."[74] He saw that Rauschenbusch's understanding of the purpose of Christianity was to make an ancient heritage relevant to the dominant social concern of the present. This was in keeping with Rauschenbusch's view that "Christianity is in its nature revolutionary."[75]

Nonetheless, Rauschenbusch believed that those needing redemption were not only the super-personal forces in business but also governments and political oligarchies and any other composite personalities that were involved in the Kingdom of Evil. The only way any super-personal entity could find redemption, he felt, was by that entity coming under the law of Christ. The way the super-personal forces were to come under the law of Christ he depicted in the following manner:

> The fundamental step of repentance and conversion for professions and organizations is to give up monopoly power and the incomes

derived from legalized extortion, and to come under the law of service, content with a fair income for honest work. The corresponding step in the case of governments and political oligarchies, both in monarchies and in capitalistic semi-democracies is to submit to real democracy. Therewith they step out of the Kingdom of Evil into the Kingdom of God.[76]

The Church as the Social Factor in Redemption

William Adams Brown has accused Rauschenbusch and the other liberal thinkers of his day of substituting the social gospel for the church. In Brown's opinion, Rauschenbusch gave a relatively small place in his social philosophy to the nature and functions of the church and, therefore, "in the great transformation which is needed the existing Churches are given no significant role to play."[77] There is certainly no doubt that Rauschenbusch modified and reinterpreted the role of the church in the social movement, but it is an unjust criticism to accuse him of giving the church no significant role in the transformation of society. Transformation was to begin with the church. Although Rauschenbusch was one of the church's greatest critics, he was also one of its greatest devotees. He believed that the church was "the incarnation of the Christ-spirit on earth, the organized conscience of Christendom."[78] He lifted the role of the church to a lofty position when he declared that "the Church is the permanent social factor in salvation."[79] Glenn Hinson notes that Rauschenbusch derived some of his understanding of the church from Anabaptist sectarianism as a voluntary society and the kingdom as gradually evolving. He also observes that his view of following Jesus, which ruled out selfish acquisition, was influenced by Francis of Assisi, Peter Waldo, John Wycliffe, John Wesley, and William Booth.[80]

In a sermon preached before the Northern Baptist Convention on May 8, 1910, titled "The Freedom of Spiritual Religion," Rauschenbusch asserted that the Baptist denomination began in the last grand transitional age in the Protestant Reformation under Zwingli, the most radical of the reformers Luther and Calvin. "We

THE CONCEPT OF SOCIAL REDEMPTION

were the radicals of the radicals,"[81] Rauschenbusch boldly declared. In that same sermon, he continued,

> We were for a "reformation without tarrying," even if we had to leave the old church and break it in pieces. We were against clericalism and against all hierarchies. We were for the religious emancipation of the laity. We went as far as the most radical Calvinist in purging religion of superstition, and when he stopped we went on. The others reformed the Lord's Supper, and cleared it of the abuses which had grown up about it, but they feared to attempt the reformation of baptism, for they knew that would shake the foundation of church life. The abolition of infant baptism meant not simply the modification of one church rite, but a revolutionary reconstruction of the very conception of the church.[82]

Rauschenbusch stated that our fathers paid for their understanding of the church with their blood, but history had vindicated their courageous efforts. He believed that this radical party of the Reformation was the fastest and most decided where Christianity had been allowed to follow its own genius, and that its triumph has been most complete in America.[83]

The organizational church in Rauschenbusch's opinion had become a necessity. If there had never been such an organization as the Christian Church, he believed that every great religious mind would have dreamed of the possibility of bringing something like it into creation. He realized that no great idea could last without its organizational counterpart. If evil could be organized in superpersonal entities, Rauschenbusch wondered what, then, a superpersonal entity organized around Jesus Christ as its impelling power might be able to accomplish. The church was to be this mighty entity, and its chief object was to embody the spirit of Christ and to carry him into every avenue of human thought and conduct.[84]

In his prayer for the church, Rauschenbusch wrote, "When we compare her with all other human institutions, we rejoice, for there is none like her." Continuing, he prays,

> But when we judge her by the mind of her Master, we bow in pity and contrition. . . . Bestow upon her a more imperious responsiveness to duty, a swifter compassion with suffering, and an utter loyalty to the will of God. Put upon her lips the ancient gospel of her Lord. Help her to proclaim boldly the coming of the Kingdom of God and the doom of all that resists it. Fill her with the prophet's scorn of tyranny, and with a Christ-like tenderness for the heavy-laden and down-trodden.[85]

In writing about the human agencies in Jesus' revolutionary work, Rauschenbusch affirms that Christ "established the church, and this formation of a revolutionary community is essential to his work." He continues,

> Jesus not only bound men to himself, he bound them to one another. He founded a community, created a corporate feeling which differentiated them from the mass of men, gave them laws of their own, and established the rudiments of an internal organization. He prayed for their unity. He expected them to continue in this society after his own departure.[86]

Rauschenbusch's idea of the indispensability of the church rested on his concept of solidarity. Having been influenced by the theological insights of Schleiermacher, Ritschl, and Royce, Rauschenbusch enumerated that the individual was to find salvation by membership in a community that has salvation.[87] The Christian religion has possession of such a community. "When a man becomes loyal to a community, he identifies himself with its life; he appropriates its past history and memories, its experiences and hopes, and absorbs its spirit and faith. This is the power which can lift him above his own level."[88]

Although Rauschenbusch believed that the Christian religion had possession of such a community, he did not equate this community with the church. The Church was envisioned as having saving power only so long as it continued to embody Christ. Christ was not only the initiator of the community of faith but is also to be the continued revolutionary force within it, and the church is in possession of saving qualities only when it translates the personal life of Jesus Christ into the social realm and thus is influential on the individual within the group. Rauschenbusch noted that it was historically true that churches do lose their saving power, and when they do they become assimilated with the world.[89] Drexel Brunson in his careful research on Rauschenbusch agrees that in Rauschenbusch's perspective, the church had become partially Christianized, but the process was not complete and the church had to abandon its spiritual isolation and seek its salvation in the kingdom of God.[90] "Rauschenbusch concentrated on the conversion of the Church at least as much," Joan Chittister observes, "as he concentrated on the conversion of churchgoers."[91]

Rauschenbusch believed that the changing social conditions in the world demanded that the church look away from its emphasis on life beyond this one and focus on the problems of the slums, poverty, crime, business malpractices, and unemployment. His harsh criticism of and challenge to the present church is apparent in the following:

> To become fully Christian the Church must come out of its isolation. In theory and practice the Church has long constituted a world by itself. It has been governed by ecclesiastical motives and interests, which are often remote from the interests of humanity, and has almost uniformly set church questions ahead of social questions. It has often built a sound-proof habitation in which people could live for years without becoming definitely conscious of the existence of prostitution, child labor, or tenement crowding. It has offered peace and spiritual tranquility to men and women who needed thunderclaps and lightnings. Like all the rest of us, the church will get salvation by finding the purpose of its existence outside itself, in the Kingdom of God, the perfect life of the race.[92]

Again, the central doctrine underlying all of Rauschenbusch's theology was the concept of the Kingdom of God. To him this doctrine was itself the social gospel.[93] He believed that Jesus had not intended to found an institutional church but had sought instead to establish the Kingdom of God among humanity. The actual church soon began to displace the Kingdom of God idea, and when this happened, Rauschenbusch observed that the ethical force of Christianity was weakened and replaced by sacramental worship and priestly importance. The Kingdom of God ceased to be the dominating religious force, and the church was moved into the position of supremacy. When the Kingdom ideal was replaced by the church, Rauschenbusch noted that the church gave exaggerated importance to itself and its functions, and all religious value was taken out of the services rendered to the secular community. Salvation came to be seen only in the relationship of the individual to the church without any thought of saving the social order.[94]

Rauschenbusch believed that the Kingdom of God is divine in its origin, progress, and consummation and is, therefore, miraculous all the way and is the continuous revelation of the power, righteousness, and love of God. "The establishment of a community of righteousness in mankind is just as much a saving act as the salvation of an individual from his natural selfishness and moral inability," he wrote.[95] He believed that the doctrine of the Kingdom of God was absolutely necessary for establishing the organic unity between theology and ethics. "Without this doctrine we shall have expositions of schemes of redemption and we shall have systems of ethics, but we shall not have a true exposition of Christianity."[96]

The church is not to exist for its own sake but is to strive to create the Kingdom of God among humanity. The spiritual authority and honor of the church are to be measured by the manner in which it fulfills this purpose.

> The institutions of the Church, its activities, its worship, and its theology must in the long run be tested by its effectiveness in creating the Kingdom of God. For the Church to see itself apart from the Kingdom, and to find its aim in itself, is the same sin of selfish detachment as when an individual selfishly separates himself from the common good. The Church has the power to save in so far as the Kingdom of God is present in it. If the Church is not living for the Kingdom, its institutions are part of the "world." In that case it is not the power of redemption but its object. It may even become an anti-Christian power. If any form of church organization which formerly aided the Kingdom now impedes it, the reason for its existence is gone.[97]

Rauschenbusch saw nothing in the church that gave it sacramental power. He was very opposed to "ceremonialism," which he saw as a symptom of spiritual decay, and said that the church must be forever on watch against this intensive enemy of Christianity.[98] If the institutional church does not serve the Kingdom of God, he believed that there was no reason for its existence. Without the purpose of the Kingdom of God pulsating within her, the church could become a super-personal entity within the Kingdom of Evil.

> Religion may develop an elaborate social apparatus of its own, wheels within wheels, and instead of being a dynamic of righteousness in the natural social relations of men, its energies may be consumed in driving its own machinery. Instead of being the powerhouse supplying the Kingdom of God among men with power and light, the Church may exist for its own sake. It then may become an expensive consumer of social wealth, a conservative clog, and a real hindrance of social progress.[99]

The church can be the social factor in redemption, then, only to the degree that it embodies the Kingdom of God. The church's institutional nature, its continuity, its ordination, its ministry, or its doctrine did not in Rauschenbusch's belief give the church any saving power. Its saving power rests only on the presence of the Kingdom of God within it.[100] "Unless the Church is vitalized by the ever nascent forces of the Kingdom within her, she deadens instead of begetting."[101] Rauschenbusch wrote that "all bodies organized for moral and religious ends manifest such a frightful inclination to become corrupt." Continuing, he said, "Marks of the true church are: present spiritual power, loyalty to Jesus, an unworldly morality, seeking and saving the lost, self-sacrifice and self-crucifixion."[102] Winthrop Hudson observed that the churches honored Rauschenbusch "as a prophet, with applause and denunciation, but they went their way quite oblivious to his sober words of warning and rebuke." "The churches, victims of their own complacency," he continued, "had first to embrace the world and demonstrate the folly of their waywardness, before they could be recalled to an awareness of their own distinctive vocation in society."[103]

In his 1918 Lyman Beecher Lectures at Yale University, titled "In a Day of Social Rebuilding," Henry Sloane Coffin, minister at the Madison Avenue Presbyterian Church and associate professor in Union Theological Seminary in New York City, spoke about how the church was shown to be powerless to build a social order. "The chief criticism of the Church preceding the war [World War I] was the insignificance of its influence upon social relations," he noted, echoing Rauschenbusch's criticism. "While there was much talk of the social gospel, the fact remained that many of the most socially-minded men and women had ceased to look to the Christian Church as a source of inspiration."[104] Few in society, he felt, were aware of the real contents of the Christian faith that would summon people to look to the church for leadership in social rebuilding. Many of the leaders of churches, he observed, were more focused on maintaining the organizations and machinery of their churches than giving life to the society in which they lived.[105]

In 1902, an earlier Lyman Beecher Lectures series titled "Social Salvation" was presented by Washington Gladden, minister of the First Congregational Church in Columbus, Ohio, and a pioneer in the social gospel movement. Gladden challenged his listeners, mostly young men preparing for ministry, in cooperation with others in their communities, to apply the social principles he enumerated to the social problems in the social order where they lived. He did not believe that there could be any adequate social reform that did not spring from a genuine revival of religion. But it had to be, he argued, "a religion that was less concerned about getting men to heaven [an argument similar to Rauschenbusch's] than about fitting them for their proper work on earth."[106] This had to be, according to him, a religion that was not against secular life but actually entered into the secular world and subdued it by its power, ruled by its law, and transfigured society by its light.[107]

Rauschenbusch did not believe that the Kingdom of God could be confined within the limitations of the church. He saw the Kingdom of God as embracing every area of human life and as the force that was to bring about the transfiguration of the social order. He saw the church as only one social institution alongside the family, the industrial organizations, the state, and all the other social organizations, and felt that the Kingdom of God was to be a realizable force in all of them.[108] "The Church is indispensable to the religious education of humanity and to the conservation of religion, but the greatest future awaits religion in the public life of humanity."[109] In interpreting Rauschenbusch's teaching, Rosemary Ruether wrote that the freedom and fellowship between people found in the church "could only be fulfilled by the extension of democratic participation to all spheres of life."[110] Christopher Evans declares that Rauschenbusch's interpretation of the nature of salvation serves as a "powerful reminder that any talk of Christian missions for the next century that does not take seriously the integration between personal faith and social transformation is an incomplete vision for the church."[111]

In a summary retrospect of Rauschenbusch's concept of social redemption, one finds that he always believed that salvation was to be considered in the light of its social implications. His concept of racial solidarity provided the marrow for his view of social redemption. Nowhere is his concept of racial solidarity more clearly seen than in his doctrine of the atonement. In his opinion, the concept of solidarity provided the solution to the problem of the atonement. Jesus lived in the midst of the Kingdom of Evil, Rauschenbusch noted, and it was the public and organized evil that killed him and not merely the personal transgression of individual men who were living then. Jesus bore the collective sins of humanity, and these were seen as the social sins of all humankind; and all people who have ever lived have contributed to them, and all who have ever lived have suffered under them. The atonement was believed to affect humanity in at least three ways: it was the conclusive demonstration of the power of sin in humanity, it was the supreme revelation of love, and it reinforced prophetic religion.

Since sin was envisioned as being caused not only by individuals but also by super-personal entities, Rauschenbusch also enumerated a concept of redemption for the super-personal entities. This called for the redemption of all forces that were not under the law of Christ, especially business. The church was seen as the social factor in redemption. It was not depicted as having a sacramental nature in itself and was not equated by Rauschenbusch with the Kingdom of God. The institutional church can be the social factor in redemption only to the degree that it embodies the Kingdom of God. Without the pulsating force of the Kingdom of God within her, the church is only another force in society that needs to be brought under the law of Christ.

Even with his criticism of the church, Rauschenbusch still affirmed, "I have full faith in the future of the Christian church."[112] He summoned the church to move away from the old evangelism of the past with its distorted, powerless, individualistic concept to the new evangelism that opens our minds to "the Spirit of Jesus in its primitive, uncorrupted and still unexhausted power." He called this Spirit the "fountain of youth" for the church that would rejuvenate it by a new baptism in that Spirit and provide its own appropriation and understanding of the gospel.[113] "Our bitter need will drive us to repentance. The prophetic Spirit will awaken among us," he proclaimed. "The tongue of fire will descend on twentieth century men and give them great faith, joy and boldness, and then we shall hear the new evangel, and it will be the Old Gospel."[114]

Notes

1. Christopher H. Evans, *The Kingdom Is Always but Coming: A Life of Walter Rauschenbusch* (Grand Rapids MI: William B. Eerdmans Publishing Co., 2004) xxvii.

2. WR, *The Righteousness of the Kingdom*, ed. Max L. Stackhouse (Nashville: Abingdon Press, 1968) 110–11.

3. WR, *A Theology for the Social Gospel* (New York: Macmillan Company, 1917) 167.

4. WR, *Unto Me* (New York: Pilgrim Press, 1912) 16–17.

5. WR, *Christianity and Social Crisis* (New York: Macmillan Company, 1907) 48.

6. WR, *Prayers of the Social Awakening* (New York: Pilgrim Press, 1910) 23.

7. Waldo Beach and H. Richard Niebuhr, eds., *Christian Ethics* (New York: Ronald Press Company, 1955) 447.

8. WR, *A Theology for the Social Gospel*, 48.

9. WR, *The Social Principles of Jesus* (New York: Association Press, 1917) 163.

10. WR, *Christianity and the Social Crisis*, 367.

11. Ibid., 65–66.

12. WR, *Christianizing the Social Order* (New York: Macmillan Company, 1912) 464–65.

13. WR, *Christianity and the Social Crisis*, 340.

14. WR, *A Theology for the Social Gospel*, 97.

15. I. M. Haldeman, *Professor Rauschenbusch's Christianity and the Social Crisis* (New York: Charles C. Cook, 1911) 29–30.

16. WR, *Christianizing the Social Order*, 56.

17. George M. Marsden, *Fundamentalism and American Culture: The Shaping of Twentieth Century Evangelicalism, 1870–1925* (New York: Oxford University Press, 1980) 92.

18. Ibid.

19. WR, *Christianity and the Social Crisis*, 106.

20. Ibid., 90.

21. WR, *Christianizing the Social Order*, 116.

22. WR, *A Theology for the Social Gospel*, 244.

23. Evans, *The Kingdom Is Always but Coming*, 39.

24. Ibid., 245.

25. In Benson Y. Landis (comp.), *A Rauschenbusch Reader* (New York: Harper and Brothers, 1957) 134

26. WR, *A Theology for the Social Gospel*, 245.

27. Ibid., 245–46.

28. Ibid., 247.

29. Ibid., 248–58.

30. Ibid., 258–59.

31. Ibid., 259.

32. Ibid.

33. Ibid., 260–61.

34. Ibid., 264.

35. Ibid., 264–65.

36. Ibid., 266.

37. Ibid., 267.

38. Ibid., 268.

39. Ibid., 270–73.

40. Ibid., 273.

41. Ibid., 274–79.

42. Evans, *The Kingdom Is Always but Coming*, 79. See H. Richard Niebuhr, *The Kingdom of God in America* (New York: Harper, 1937) 184ff.

43. Niebuhr, *Kingdom of God in America*, 194.

44. WR, *A Theology for the Social Gospel*, 226.

45. WR, *The Social Principles of Jesus*, 167ff.

46. Ibid., 175.

47. *The Rochester Theological Seminary Record*, November 1918, p. 42.

48. WR, *A Theology for the Social Gospel*, 69.

49. Ibid., 70–71.

50. Ibid., 75–76.

51. Ibid., 72.

52. Ibid., 110.

53. Ibid., 111.

54. David Bryan True, "Faith Politics: The Tradition of Martin Luther King, Jr., Reinhold Niebuhr, and Walter Rauschenbusch," unpublished PhD diss., Union Theological Seminary and Presbyterian School of Christian Education, Richmond VA, December 2005, p. 54.

55. WR, *Christianizing the Social Order*, 154.

56. Ibid., 155.

57. Ross Douthat, *Bad Religion: How We Became a Nation of Heretics* (New York: Free Press, 2012) 28.

58. Frederick Sontag and John K. Roth, *The American Religious Experience: The Roots, Trends, and Future of Theology* (New York: Harper & Row, Publishers, 1972) 140, their italics.

59. WR, *Christianity and the Social Crisis*, 346.

60. WR, *A Theology for the Social Gospel*, 226.

61. WR, *Christianity and the Social Crisis*, 420–21.

62. Ibid., 279.

63. F. Ernest Johnson, *The Social Gospel Re-Examined* (New York: Harper & Brothers, 1940) 93–94.

64. Rosemary Radford Ruether, *The Radical Kingdom: The Western Experience of Messianic Hope* (New York: Harper & Row, Publishers, 1970) 84.

65. WR, *Christianity and the Social Crisis*, 285.

66. Stanley Hauerwas, *Dispatches from the Front: Theological Engagements with the Secular* (Durham NC: Duke University Press, 1994) 97.

67. WR, *Christianity and the Social Crisis*, 210.

68. William A. Mueller, "The Life, Work and Gospel of Walter Rauschenbusch," *Religion in Life* 15 (Autumn 1946): 537–38.

69. WR, *Christianizing the Social Order*, 156.

70. WR, *Christianity and the Social Crisis*, 372.

71. WR, *Christianizing the Social Order*, 156.

72. Ibid., 222–34, 311–23, 332–40. See also WR, *A Theology for the Social Gospel*, 19.

73. Martin E. Marty, *Modern American Religion: The Irony of It All, 1893–1919*, vol. 1 (Chicago: University of Chicago Press, 1986) 286–97.

74. Christopher H. Evans, ed., *The Social Gospel Today* (Louisville: Westminster John Knox Press, 2001) 4.

75. WR, *The Righteousness of the Kingdom*, 79

76. Rauschenbusch, *Christianizing the Social Order*, 117.

77. In David E. Roberts and Henry P. Van Dusen, eds., *Liberal Theology: An Appraisal* (New York: Charles Scribner's Sons, 1942) 260.

78. WR, *Christianity and the Social Crisis*, 287.

79. WR, *The Social Principles of Jesus*, 164.

80. Glenn Hinson, "Baptists and the Social Gospel and the Turn toward Social Justice: 1898–1917," in Michael E. Williams, Sr., and Walter Shurden, eds., *Turning Points in Baptist History: A Festschrift in Honor of Harry Leon McBeth* (Macon GA: Mercer University Press, 2008) 245–46.

81. WR, "The Freedom of Spiritual Religion," Philadelphia, 1910, sermon transcript, p. 12. Quoted in Don E. Smucker, "Walter Rauschenbush and the Anabaptist Historiography," *The Recovery of the Anabaptist Vision*, ed. Guy F. Hershberger (Scottdale PA: Herald Press, 1957) 296.

82. Smucker, *The Recovery of the Anabaptist Vision*, 297.

83. Ibid., 297–98.

84. WR, *A Theology for the Social Gospel*, 119–20.

85. WR, *Prayers of the Social Awakening* (Boston: Pilgrim Press, 1910) 119–20.

86. WR, *The Righteousness of the Kingdom*, ed. Max L. Stackhouse (Nashville: Abingdon Press, 1968) 151.

87. Ibid., 125–26.

88. Ibid., 126–27.

89. Ibid., 128.

90. Drexel Timothy Brunson, "The Quest for Social Justice: A Study of Walter Rauschenbusch and His Influence on Reinhold Niebuhr and Martin Luther King, Jr.," PhD diss., Florida State University, December 1980, p. 99.

91. Joan Chittister, "Unless the Call Be Heard Again," in WR, *Christianity and the Social Crisis for the 21st Century* (New York: HarperOne, 2007) 119.

92. In Anna M. Singer, *Walter Rauschenbusch and His Contribution to Social Christianity* (Boston: Richard G. Badger, 1920), quoted in O. K. Armstrong and Marjorie M. Armstrong, *The Indomitable Baptists: A Narrative of Their Role in Shaping American History* (Garden City NY: Doubleday & Company, Inc., 1967) 202.

93. WR, *The Righteousness of the Kingdom*, 131.

94. Ibid., 131–37. See also WR, *Christianity and the Social Crisis*, 179–86.

95. WR, *The Righteousness of the Kingdom*, 139–40.

96. Ibid., 140.

97. Ibid., 143–44.

98. WR, *The Righteousness of the Kingdom*, 272–73.

99. WR, *The Social Principles of Jesus*, 142.

100. WR, *A Theology for the Social Gospel*, 129.

101. Ibid., 130.

102. WR, in *The Examiner*, 28 July 1892, quoted in August Hopkins Strong, *Systematic Theology*, 3 vols. in 1 (Philadelphia: Judson Press, 1907) 909–10.

103. Winthrop Hudson, *The Great Tradition of the American Churches* (New York: Harper & Brothers, 1953) 242.

104. Henry Sloane Coffin, *In a Day of Social Rebuilding* (New Haven: Yale University Press, 1918) 6.

105. Ibid., 6–9.

106. Washington Gladden, *Social Salvation* (Boston: Houghton Mifflin, 1902; repr. Eugene OR: Wipf and Stock Publishers, 2004) 30.

107. Ibid.

108. WR, *A Theology for the Social Gospel*, 144–45.

109. Ibid., 145.

110. Rosemary Radford Ruether, *The Radical Kingdom: The Western Experience of Messianic Hope* (New York: Harper & Row, Publishers, 1970) 85.

111. Christopher H. Evans, ed., *The Social Gospel Today* (Louisville: Westminster John Knox Press, 2001) 7.

112. WR, "The New Evangelism," *The Independent* 61 (January–June 1940): 1054–59, quoted in *Walter Rauschenbusch: Selected Writings*, ed. Winthrop S. Hudson (New York: Paulist Press, 1984) 144.

113. Ibid., 143–44.

114. Ibid., 144.

Chapter 7

Summary and Conclusion

A Brief Summary of Rauschenbusch's Theology

The social gospel movement originated as a reaction against the individualistic emphasis of orthodox Christianity. The emphasis on personal salvation without any social implications and the extreme futuristic concern were repudiated by the advocates of the social gospel. Certain types of nineteenth-century problems such as unrestricted competition of economics, the conflict between labor and capital, business ethics, and the problems of urban life accentuated the development of social concern. The social gospel was an indigenous American movement that was influenced by the age in which it was born. Probably the greatest factor in the development of the social gospel was the intensity of the social problems themselves, but the influence of Puritan theology, the contribution of the enlightenment and revivalism, and the influence of the physical sciences, evolution, and liberal theology contributed to the incipience of the social movement. The social gospel movement awakened American Protestantism to a new emphasis in Christianity.

From a brief sketch of Rauschenbusch's life, it has been shown that his concepts of sin and salvation were not the products of abstract speculation but were forged on the anvil of his personal experience with the "heartbeat" of humanity. The eleven years that he served as pastor to the poverty-stricken congregation situated on the edge of "Hell's Kitchen," one of New York City's notorious slums, made a profound impression on his mind and led him to an awareness of the necessity for a social application of the gospel. His wide reading in social philosophy and theology strengthened his social concern.

Through his teaching, speaking engagements, and writings he was soon recognized as the foremost spokesman in American social Christianity. A brief sketch of Rauschenbusch's life has revealed the integral part his personal acquaintance with the social forces of evil played in the evolution of his concept of redemption.

Rauschenbusch had witnessed the power of evil in his concrete relationship with humanity, especially in his eleven years in "Hell's Kitchen," and therefore his concept of sin was grounded in firm reality. He acknowledged that humanity by its very nature is involved in sin and that one needs to be brought to the realization of his or her predicament. Rauschenbusch discerned the nature of sin as essentially selfishness, and he depicted humanity's rebellion against God not as a solitary duel of the will between mortals and God but as a relationship that always includes humanity. He accepted sin as rebellion against God but not in the sense of a lone person isolated from the world repudiating the will of God. He believed that a man or woman rarely sins against God alone. Humanity is always involved in one's relationship to God. Therefore, man or woman's sins against the least of his or her fellow persons concern God.

Original sin was the concept that Rauschenbusch used to depict the transmission of sin from generation to generation. The doctrine of original sin was to him a social concept. Traditional theology, he thought, had overlooked the fact that sin was transmitted along the lines of social tradition and assimilation as well as by biological propagation. He was concerned with much more than just the influence of evil examples; he was concerned with the spiritual authority exercised by society over its members. Because the transmission of sin was understood as social and interpreted not as the result of a remote event in the past, he believed that the ethical and religious forces could do something to check and prevent the transmission of original sin.

The advance of the Kingdom of God was depicted as coming only by conflict with the Kingdom of Evil. Each person has personally contributed to the Kingdom of Evil by his or her personal sins, and the first requirement of the social gospel is for each person to repent of those personal sins. Rauschenbusch in no way sought to minimize personal sin, and he clearly stated that man and woman's first step into the Kingdom of God could come only after personal repentance. But he also emphasized that sin is never simply a private matter, and therefore man or woman needs to realize his or her solidaristic involvement with mortals in collective sin. The sin of one person affects all, and the sin of all affects each individual in society. Because of the collective nature of sin, he felt that there were super-personal forces of evil that needed to come under the law of Christ. These super-personal forces were entities beyond the individual like social organizations, clubs, gangs, economic systems, states, etc. The solidaristic spiritual concept of sin converged into the doctrine of the Kingdom of Evil. The social gospel was believed to be the only influence that had an adequate view of the solidarity of humanity and that had a sufficient understanding of the social realities of sin to be able to combat them.

Rauschenbusch believed that there was more involved in the reality of sin than merely human frailty and stupidity and bad influences; he felt that there existed a permanent force of organized evil. This force of organized evil in his opinion could no longer be considered a demonic power. Satan and his devils were interpreted as a fading religious entity. Rauschenbusch called for a reevaluation of the belief in a satanic kingdom based on political and social factors. He interpreted the devil as a picturesque term used to denote the personification of evil forces that were seen objectified in business, war, tyranny, and any other force that negated the intrinsic worth of humanity.

In his emphasis on corporate redemption, Rauschenbusch did not attempt to obliterate the necessity for personal salvation. Realizing the sacredness of every human personality, he interpreted the first requirement for entrance into the Kingdom of God as being a personal experience with God. Humanity's salvation was depicted as being engendered through a personal encounter with God and not merely as an ascent to a set of propositional truths about Christ. This personal experience freed people from any need of sacramentalism or dogmatism and was to be a free and voluntary experience. Rauschenbusch's own personal religious experience and his devotional life have also provided insight into his concept of personal redemption.

Several observations may be noted in connection with Rauschenbusch's view of personal salvation. (1) Personal redemption was not reduced to a mystical experience. The mystical way, he felt, was above humanity and not through it. He would allow only an anthropocentric mysticism that would enable people to realize the necessity of a proper relationship with fellow men and women as well as with God. Personal salvation was not interpreted in terms of subjective mysticism. (2) Asceticism and otherworldliness were seen as one of the major factors for the failure of Christianity to undertake social reconstruction. Any concept of personal redemption that placed its emphasis on removing the individual from this life and negated the significance of Christianizing the social order was, in Rauschenbusch's opinion, unrelated to the true Christian message of salvation. (3) Man/Woman did have a personal experience with God, but with this experience it was emphasized that man/woman always had to realize his/her solidaristic involvement with humanity. Man/woman was never viewed as an atomistic individual in relationship with God but was always considered in his/her relational involvement within the commonwealth of humanity. Any personal religious experience that did not have in it a relationship to one's fellow man and woman was not considered distinctively Christian. The life of humanity was seen as infinitely interwoven in its sin and salvation.

Rauschenbusch affirmed his faith in the belief in eternal life, but he did not want the belief in life after death to negate the importance of Christian action in this world. He felt that the hope of a higher life for the human race did not solve the problem for the individual person and therefore stated that a person should look for the consummation of labor in an existence after death. Rauschenbusch's view of eternal life has clearly revealed a concept of universal salvation. The idea of an immediate fixity of two states after death was rejected, and he offered, instead, the idea of an ascending scale toward God reaching from the lowest to the highest in which each person would have his or her place according to his or her own spiritual growth obtained in this life. His view of an ascending scale depicted a mortal as being in as much darkness and narrowness as that person deserved by one's life on earth but allowing always for the possibility of growth.

No one was either "saved" or "damned" completely. In the ascending scale of being, no one was pictured so high that he or she could not still be drawn closer to God and no one so low that he or she could be beyond God's love. God was depicted as one who would *always* be teaching and saving *all* people. Punishment was to be educational and redemptive, not vindictive.

Rauschenbusch's concept of universal salvation did not grow out of a view of "love mysticism." It was the only ultimate solution he saw that would not reduce God to a "finite" being or instate evil as the final victor over righteousness. He had seen sin as a grim reality, and he realized the great power of the Kingdom of Evil; but he stated firmly that good ultimately would triumph over evil. An eternal hell would indicate that God was not able ultimately to overcome evil with good, and Rauschenbusch could not believe this. His concept of universal salvation was based on a vivid awareness of the power of sin and a vivid awareness of the power of God. His concept of an ascending scale was the way he sought to satisfy both God's justice and God's love.

Rauschenbusch always emphasized the moral aspect of salvation. In his opinion, the church's eyes should be moved from the far distant "clouds" to the realization that the Christian's aim was not so much to pass through this world safely to those "clouds," leaving the world's evil unshaken, as it was to seek a religious and moral transformation of humanity in this life's walk. He viewed religion and ethics as inseparable. No one could claim to have "faith" in God and repudiate the moral law. Love to God was interpreted as inseparable from love to other people. No one could love God who did not express it in his or her love to fellow men and women. Salvation was always interpreted as carrying with it social implications.

In considering Rauschenbusch's doctrine of sin, it is seen that he believed the responsibility for sin lay not only on the individual person but also on forces that he called super-personal entities. These super-personal forces such as political parties, business organizations, social groups, and other combinations of individuals needed to come under the law of Christ if they were to be redeemed. He saw four sections of our country as being already Christianized: the family, the organized religious life, the institution of education, and the political organization of the nation. This seems to be an unrealistic optimism, and one wonders if Rauschenbusch would seek to maintain such a position if he were alive today. The concept of super-personal forces, however, should still be emphasized today in order to bring people to the realization of their collective responsibility for any organization or group in which they are active participants.

The concept of racial solidarity provided the solution in Rauschenbusch's opinion for an understanding of the doctrine of the atonement. He felt that Jesus did not bear humanity's sins by imputation because guilt and merit were conceived as personal and not transferable from one person to another. Imputation was seen as merely a legal device to enable the law to hold another person responsible for a crime committed by someone else. He felt that it had been the public and organized evil that had killed Jesus and not simply the personal sins of individuals. Jesus bore the collective sins of humanity, and all people who have ever lived have contributed to them and have suffered under them. These collective sins were listed as religious bigotry, the combination of graft and political power, the corruption of justice, the mob spirit, militarism, and class contempt. By repeating the sins of the past, one is involved in the guilt of the past. All humanity was seen as being linked in solidarity of evil and guilt.

The spiritual and redemptive value of the death of Jesus was regarded not in the quantity of his mental and physical suffering but in his willingness to take upon himself the highest and hardest part of his life's work. The death of Jesus was interpreted as being an integral part of his life. The whole life of Jesus was seen as being given in love and service, and his death was seen as having the same significance. His death was the culmination of his life's work and its most luminous part. By his death, Jesus revealed dramatically what he had been teaching in his life.

The atonement was believed to affect humanity in at least three ways: (1) it was the conclusive demonstration of the power of sin in humanity; (2) as the death of Jesus, it was the supreme revelation of love; and (3) it served to reinforce prophetic religion and was the clearest and most conspicuous instance of prophetic suffering. Those who have to bear prophetic suffering can receive comfort from the fact that they are carrying on what Jesus has done.

The church was interpreted as the social factor in redemption. It is indispensable in the sense that it possesses a community that has salvation. But Rauschenbusch did not equate the church with this spiritual community. The church was seen as the social factor in redemption only to the degree that it embodied the Kingdom of God. Neither the church's institutional nature, its continuity, its ordination, its ministry, nor its doctrines gives the church any saving power. He believed that the church has a significant role in society, but he felt that when the church is content to spend its time propagating itself instead of the Kingdom of God, then it too needs to be Christianized. The church's "saving power" rests on the pulsating power of the Kingdom of God within her. The Kingdom of God was not interpreted as being confined within the limitations of the institutional church but was to be realized within the family, the industrial organizations, the state, and all other social organizations. All of society was to be Christianized.

The Kingdom of God was the concept that Rauschenbusch used to depict the Christianization of society. It was his soteriological term that expressed his conviction in social redemption. His basic theological emphasis was, therefore, soteriological, the personal salvation of man and woman, and the corporate redemption of society.

Strengths of Rauschenbusch's Theology[1]

1. His belief in the social gospel was undergirded by his own deep personal faith. His theology was not based on abstract speculation but arose out of his personal religious experience. Religion was a vital experience for him. "A great task," he said, "demands a great faith." Although Rauschenbusch rejected mysticism, his own religious experience seemed mystical in its rootage. In humility, he concluded his book on prayer with his own prayer: "Pardon the frailty of thy servant, and look upon him only as he sinks his life in Jesus, his Master and Saviour. Amen."[2]

2. Rauschenbusch was a prophet who called the church to reexamine its theology and see the solidarity of the human race. He

declared that sin is not merely a personal matter but affects society as well. Salvation, likewise, is concerned not just with "saving souls" but also with redeeming the social evils of society. Social sins have to be eradicated as well as individual sins.

3. Faith is not a private matter but involves others. Rauschenbusch called Christians away from isolated, private religion and helped them to see their interrelatedness with others.

4. He focused the church's eyes once again on the Kingdom of God. He drew upon the central teaching of Jesus and challenged the church to model itself after the Kingdom of God and not the world. He reminded the church that it was not equated with the Kingdom of God and does not exist for its own sake.

5. He also broke down the barrier between the sacred and the secular. He always emphasized the moral dimension of salvation. Salvation could not be limited to life in church, but it addressed one's entire life—private, social, business, recreation—and all walks of life. The Christian was to be the "force" in society that labored to bring about the religious and moral transformation of humanity in the battle against the Kingdom of Evil. Religion and ethics were united in this struggle. No person could attest to a personal "faith" in God and not be concerned about the moral law. Salvation was personal but always, if authentic, not private; instead, it was concerned about the social implications of salvation for the secular world in which people live.

6. The church was reminded that it was the friend and advocate of the voiceless poor and underprivileged people in society. Following the example of its Lord, the church is called to serve and not be served and to minister to the outcast and needy in society. To ignore the hurting and helpless people in the world is to reject the call of the church's Lord to follow in his steps. The church was challenged to be the instrument to lead men and women to personal faith and to be advocates in bringing about the redemption of the Kingdom of Evil—the social order.

7. Rauschenbusch united evangelistic concern for personal redemption with concern for social reconstruction. Genuine religion was not either social action or evangelism. It affected both dimensions. Religion was to transform both individuals and society.

8. Rauschenbusch was among many religious leaders who helped found the Federal Council of Churches in 1908, which some have called "the lengthened shadow of Rauschenbusch." A "social creed of the Churches" was adopted at the first meeting of this new organization. It gave a long list of concerns for which the church was to stand. Among them were the rights of workers to protection from hardships, principles of conciliation and arbitration in industrial dissensions, the abolition of child labor, the need for a living wage, the abatement of poverty, and others.[3] The Federal Council became a sort of laboratory for the Protestant churches' new ideas, especially in social ethics, to be considered. The Federal Council of Churches became the birthfather to the National Council of Churches.

9. The shadow of Rauschenbusch has continued to fall across the path of many people through the years. As I indicated earlier, several noted people have acknowledged their indebtedness to him, including Harry Emerson Fosdick,[4] Reinhold Niebuhr, Martin Luther King, Jr.,[5] Kagawa, John Haynes Holmes, Francis J. McConnell, and countless others.[6] The recent biographies by Paul Minus and Christopher Evans and the collections of Rauschenbusch's writings by Winthrop Hudson, the latest volume on *Baptist Theologians* by George and Dockery, William Ramsay's *Four Modern Prophets*, and other recent writings indicate the continued importance of his life and theology.

Weaknesses Noted in Rauschenbusch's Theology

As significant as Rauschenbusch's contributions were to American Christianity, his theology does obviously contain some weaknesses. The most notable are the following.

1. Although Rauschenbusch acknowledged the difficulty of trying to Christianize society, he had a much too optimistic attitude toward humanity and the inevitability of human progress. He could not, nor would he today, make such an observation as, "The largest and hardest part of the work of Christianizing the social order has been done." World War I occurred shortly before he died and ended his optimism. Although Rauschenbusch's idealism has often been listed as his greatest fault, it may be, according to Gary Dorrien, his "most exemplary feature

for the modern church."[7] His idealism, according to Dorrien, resounded the cry that all movements for social progress need an energizing vision of a better world to embrace a biblical image of social and economic transformation.

2. There is a serious question of whether society can ever be fully Christianized. Social reconstruction of society cannot be equated with the Kingdom of God. Rauschenbusch seemed to believe that if certain social "disorders," like democracy, the labor movement, pacifism efforts, etc., were corrected or Christianized, then the Kingdom of God would be in a process of becoming a reality. It is evident, I believe, that the Kingdom of God will continually be in conflict with the political and social order and will not evolve into a "spiritual" realm. Christians will continue to be the salt, leaven, and light in the world, seeking to transform society, but they will most likely work gradually and inconspicuously. The Kingdom of God and the Kingdom of Evil will continue to engage in conflict.

3. Many of Rauschenbusch's specific economic remedies would be criticized today. He called himself a Christian Socialist. He believed that our society needed collective sharing, cooperation, and solidarity in the home, school, church, government, and in all of society. He advocated government ownership of railroads, the water routes, gas and electric power, and natural resources like coal mines and was clearly opposed to laissez-faire capitalism. There is no question that some of his solutions to these problems are dated, but, on the other hand, some of his suggestions have become a reality in our country, such as the federal highway system, federal laws governing the use of waterways, and minimum wage for all workers. "Rauschenbusch is dated," Max Stackhouse observes, "but he is dated for a good reason. Rauschenbusch's analysis, his suggestions, his criticisms were timely and concretely specified actions for a given era."[8]

4. His stem anti-Catholicism position reveals his opposition to priestly tradition and ceremonialism in religion. His cordial relationship with the Catholic social reformer John Ryan, however, might indicate that he would have a slightly modified position today toward the Catholic Church or some people identified with it.[9]

5. His views on women have come under criticism from feminists and others. Although Rauschenbusch believed in women's suffrage, his view of gender was locked in Victorian suppositions and his idealization of the family as a part of the Kingdom of God that had been Christianized. With his concern for all who were marginalized in society, it is likely, however, that he would have been more open to women's liberation and the equality of women today. The same could be stated in his lack of addressing the racial justice and minorities' issues of his day. These two omissions have caused some to consider the social gospel movement dated. The fact that Martin Luther King, Jr., took such support from Rauschenbusch's teachings is to me an indication that he would have been a champion of this cause today because of his concern for the poor and underprivileged. Robert McAfee Brown believes that there are affinities between liberation theology and the social movement of people like Rauschenbusch. He quotes the following lines from John C. Bennett: "Liberation theology today is in some respects in a line of succession from such representatives of the Social Gospel as Walter Rauschenbusch. The Social Gospel was a theology of liberation for the industrial workers of this country."[10]

6. His focus on this worldly order minimized the transcendence and sovereignty of God. Rauschenbusch was not concerned with a remote God. He had seen the hurt and pain of humanity around him and wrote mostly about the immanence of God. Like many correctives, his emphasis may have exaggerated one side too much.

7. Some criticism has been directed against Rauschenbusch's concept of using Jesus' view of the Kingdom of God to refer to a future Christianizing of the social order. Some of these critics would envision the Kingdom of God as beyond history; others would see it in a realized eschatology; still others would be concerned about the poor and oppressed but would not acknowledge the possibility of Christianizing the social order.

8. Although Rauschenbusch wrote about the church as the social factor in redemption, he did not seem to have a high concept of the church. The church was indispensable in the sense that it "possesses" a community that has salvation. But he did not equate the church with this spiritual community. The church was seen as the social factor in

redemption only to the degree that it embodied the Kingdom of God. The Kingdom of God was not interpreted as being confined within the limitations of the institutional church but was to be realized within the family, the industrial organizations, the state, and all other social organizations. All of society was to be Christianized. Although there is much truth in Rauschenbusch's criticism of the local church, his view seems to fall far short of the church for which Christ died and against which the gates of hell would not prevail and the Pauline image of the "Bride of Christ."

9. His view of eschatology, the life beyond, emphasized a universalism in the grace of God and seemed, in the minds of some critics, to wink at the judgment of God. Likewise, to some critics, his universalism seemed to conflict with his severe criticism of the forces of evil in this world and the power of collective evil—the Kingdom of Evil. However, to be fair with his perspective on this belief, his concept of universal salvation was based on not only what he felt was the power of sin but also on the power of God. His concept of an ascending scale was the way he sought to satisfy both God's justice and God's love.

Conclusion

In spite of some differences with Rauschenbusch's thought, his theology and ministry continue to challenge twenty-first-century Christians. "Many of Rauschenbusch's affirmations have survived merciless criticism," says Donovan E. Smucker, who has examined Rauschenbusch's thought extensively. "The blend of realism and hope, social insight and faith, divine intention and human decision is worthy of study in the perennial quest for the Christian answer to the challenge of the world and its culture."[11]

Rauschenbusch was concerned that the gospel be related to this world. He did not believe that any discussion about redemption could stop with personal redemption. Redemption also encompassed our fellow brothers and sisters, and the institutions and collective forces in society as well. If a person has been a victim of these institutions, genuine salvation does not occur until these institutions are changed. Rauschenbusch's poetic writing style and his vision of the Christianizing of society can be seen in his beautiful rendering of 1 Corinthians 13:

If I create wealth beyond the dream of past ages and increase not love, my heat is the flush of fever and my success will deal death.

Though I have foresight to locate the fountains of riches, and power to preempt them, and skill to tap them, and have no loving vision for humanity, I am blind.

Though I give of my profits to the poor and make princely endowments for those who toil for me, if I have no human fellowship of love with them, my life is barren and doomed.

Love is just and kind. Love is not greedy and covetous. Love exploits no one; it takes no unearned gain; it gives more than it gets. Love does not break down the lives of others to make wealth for itself; it makes wealth to build the life of all. Love seeks solidarity; it tolerates no divisions; it prefers equal workmates; it shares its efficiency. Love enriches all men, educates all men, and gladdens all men.

The values created by love never fail; but whether there are class privileges, they shall fail; whether there are millions gathered, they shall be scattered; and whether there are vested rights, they shall be abolished. For in the past strong men lorded it in ruthlessness and strove for their own power and pride, but when the perfect social order comes, the strong shall serve the common good. Before the sun of Christ brought in the dawn, men competed, and forced tribute from weakness, but when the full day shall come, they will work as mates in love, each for all and all for each. For now we see in the fog of selfishness, darkly, but then with social vision; now we see our fragmentary ends, but then we shall see the destinies of the race as God sees them. But now abideth honor, justice, and love, these three; and the greatest of these is love.[12]

In one of his prayers, Rauschenbusch wrote,

Cast down the throne of mammon whoever grinds the life of men and set up thy throne, O Christ, for thou doest die that men might live. Show their erring children at last the way from the city of destruction to the city of love and fulfill the longings of the prophets of humanity. Our master once more we make thy faith our prayer. Thy kingdom come, thy will be done on earth.[13]

Rauschenbusch was indeed one of the great social and religious prophets of our American heritage. He, like all prophets, will have his weaknesses, but he is a voice that the Christian church and society need to hear again in his radical call to discipleship. He will continue to be a figure that Baptists and other religious perspectives cannot ignore as they study and examine their history and those that influenced who they are.

Notes

1. Some material in this section is adapted from my chapter on Rauschenbusch in *Modern Shapers of Baptist Thought in America* (Richmond VA: Center for Baptist Heritage & Studies, 2012) 49–53.

2. WR, *Prayers of the Social Awakening* (Boston: The Pilgrim Press, 1910) 126.

3. John Robert T. Handy, ed., *The Social Gospel in America, 1870–1920* (New York: Oxford University Press, 1966) 13.

4. Harry Emerson Fosdick, *The Living of These Days* (New York: Harper and Brothers, 1956) 109.

5. Martin Luther King, Jr., "Pilgrimage to Non-Violence," *The Christian Century* 77 (13 April 1960): 440.

6. Dores Robinson Sharpe, *Walter Rauschenbusch* (New York: The Macmillan Company, 1942) 417.

7. Gary J. Dorrien, *Reconstructing the Common Good: Theology and the Social Order* (Maryknoll NY: Orbis Books, 1990) 42.

8. Max L. Stackhouse, "Eschatology and Ethical Method: A Structural Analysis of Contemporary Christian Social Ethics in America with primary reference to Walter Rauschenbusch and Reinhold Niebuhr," unpublished PhD dissertation, 1964, p. 121, quoted in Robert T. Handy, *The Social Gospel in America, 1870–1920* (New York: Oxford University Press, 1966) 262.

9. Christopher H. Evans, *The Kingdom Is Always but Coming: A Life of Walter Rauschenbusch* (Grand Rapids MI: William B. Eerdmans Publishing Co., 2004; repub., Waco TX: Baylor University Press, 2009) 210.

10. John C. Bennett, "Fitting the Liberation Theme into Our Theological Agenda," *Christianity and Crisis*, 18 July 1977, p. 167, quoted in Robert McAfee Brown, *Theology in a New Key: Responding to Liberation Themes* (Philadelphia: Westminster Press, 1978) 140.

11. Donovan E. Smucker, *The Origins of Walter Rauschenbusch's Social Ethics* (Buffalo: McGill-Queen's University Press, 1994) 8.

12. WR, *Dare We Be Christians?* (Boston: Pilgrim Press, 1914) 46–48.
13. WR, *Prayers of the Social Awakening*, 108.

Bibliography

A. Primary Sources

1. Books

Rauschenbusch, August, and Walter. *Life and Ministry of August Rauschenbusch.* Translated by Donald H. Madvig. Sioux Fall SD: Sisson Printing, Inc., 2008. Original German version, *Leben und Wirken von August Rauschenbusch,* published by Cleveland OH: German Baptist Publishing Society, 1901. (Walter drew from his father's rough drafts of several chapters, journals, and correspondence to update and complete his father's autobiography.)

Rauschenbusch, Walter. *Christianity and the Social Crisis.* New York: The Macmillan Company, 1907.

———. *Christianizing the Social Order.* New York: The Macmillan Company, 1912.

———. *Dare We Be Christians?* Boston: The Pilgrim Press, 1914.

———. *Das Leben Jesu: Ein sytematisher Studiengang fur Jugendvereine und Bibelklassen.* Cleveland: P. Ritter, 1895.

———. *Die politische Verfassung unseres (Civil Government of the United States): Ein Handbuch zum Unterrichte fur die deutschamerikanische Jugend.* Cleveland: P. Ritter, 1902.

———. *Evangeliums-Lieder 1 und 2,* with Ira D. Sankey. New York: Biglow and Main, 1897.

———. *Evangeliums-Sanger 3, 150 Neue Lieder fur abendgottesdienste und besondere versammlungen,* with Ira D. Sankey. Kassel: J. G. Oncken, 1907.

———. *Neue Lieder,* with Ira D. Sankey. Authorized translation of *Gospel Hymns Number 5,* New York: Biglow and Main, 1889.

———. *Prayers of the Social Awakening.* New York: The Pilgrim Press, 1910.

———. *A Theology for the Social Gospel.* New York: The Macmillan Company, 1917.

———. *The Righteousness of the Kingdom.* Edited and introduced by Max L. Stackhouse. Nashville: Abingdon Press, 1968. Revised edition published by Lewiston: Edwin Mellen Press, 1999.

———. *The Social Principles of Jesus.* New York: Association Press, 1917.

———. *Unto Me.* New York: The Pilgrim Press, 1912.

2. Articles

Rauschenbusch, Walter. "Christian Socialism," *A Dictionary of Religion and Ethics*, Shailer Mathews and G. B. Smith, editors, New York: The Macmillan Company, 1922, 90-91.

———. "The Church and Social Crisis." *The Baptist World Alliance: Record of Proceedings.* New York: Harper and Brothers, 1911. 373–76.

———. "The Conservation of the Social Service Message." *Messages of the Men and Religion Movement.* Volume 2 of Social Service (7 volumes). New York: Funk and Wagnalls Company, 1912. 101–25.

———. "Ideals of Social Reformers." *The American Journal of Sociology* 2 (September 1896): 202–19.

———. "The Influence of Historical Studies on Theology." *The American Journal of Theology* 11 (January 1907): 111–27.

———. "Jesus as an Organizer of Men." *The Biblical World* 10 (August 1898): 102–11.

———. The New Evangelism." *The Independent* 56 (12 May 1904): 1056–61.

———. "Revelation: An Exposition." *The Biblical World* 10 (August 1897): 94–103.

———. "The Rights of the Child in the Community." *Religious Education* 10 (June 1915): 219–25.

———. "The Social Background, Spirit and Message of the Bible." *The Rochester Theological Seminary Record* (November 1918): 54–63.

———. "The Stake of the Church in the Social Movement." *The American Journal of Sociology* 3 (July 1987): 18–30.

———. "The True American Church." *The Rochester Theological Seminary Record* (November 1918): 64–66.

———. "Why I Am a Baptist." In *A Baptist Treasury*, edited by Sydnor L. Stealey. New York: Thomas Y. Crowell Company, 1958. 163–84.

———. "The Zürick Anabaptists and Thomas Münzer." *The American Journal of Theology* 9 (January 1905): 91–106.

(For an extensive listing of Rauschenbusch's published articles, pamphlets, and reviews see Walter Rauschenbusch, *The Righteousness of the Kingdom*, ed. Max L. Stackhouse [Nashville, Abingdon, 1968] 291ff; revised and republished by Lewiston: Edwin Mellen Press, 1999. Also see Donovan E. Smucker, *The Origins of Walter Rauschenbusch's Social Ethics* [Buffalo: McGill-Queen's University Press, 1994] 159, 166f.)

B. Books Containing Both Primary and Secondary Sources

Beach, Waldo, and H. Richard Niebuhr, editors. *Christian Ethics*. New York: The Ronald Press Company, 1955.

Fant, Jr., Clyde E., and William M. Pinson. *20 Centuries of Great Preaching*. Volume 7. Waco TX: Word Books Publisher, 1971.

Ferm, Vergilius, editor. *Classics of Protestantism*. New York: Philosophical Library, 1959.

Handy, Robert T, editor. *The Social Gospel in America, 1870–1920*. New York: Oxford University Press, 1966.

Hudson, Winthrop S., editor. *Walter Rauschenbusch: Selected Writings.* New York: Paulist Press, 1984.

Humphreys, Fisher, editor. *Nineteenth Century Evangelical Theology.* Nashville: Broadman Press, 1983.

Landis, Benson Y., editor. *A Rauschenbusch Reader*, New York: Harper and Brothers, 1957.

Mays, Benjamin E., compiler. *A Gospel for the Social Awakening.* New York: Association Press, 1950.

Pelikan, Jaroslav W., editor. *The World's Treasury of Modern Religious Thought.* Boston: Little, Brown and Company, 1990.

Rauschenbusch, Walter. *Christianity and the Social Crisis for the 21st Century.* New York: HarperOne, 2007.

The Rochester Theological Seminary Record (The Rauschenbusch Number), Rochester NY, November 1918.

Stuber, Stanley Irving, compiler and editor. *Basic Christian Writings.* New York: Association Press, 1957.

———, compiler. *The Christian Reader: Inspirational and Devotional Classics.* New York: Association Press, 1955.

C. Secondary Sources

1. Books

Armstrong, O. K., and Marjorie M. Armstrong. *The Indomitable Baptists: A Narrative of Their Role in Shaping American History.* Garden City NY: Doubleday & Company, Inc., 1967.

Atkins, Gaius G. *Religion in Our Time.* New York: Round Table Press, Inc., 1932.

Bass, Archer B. *Protestantism in the United States.* New York: Thomas Y. Crowell Company, 1929.

Beckley, Harlan. *Passion for Justice: Retrieving the Legacies of Walter Rauschenbusch, John A. Ryan, and Reinhold Niebuhr.* Louisville: Westminster/ John Knox Press, 1992.

Bennett, John C. *Social Salvation*. New York: Charles Scribner's Sons, 1948.

Bodein, Vernon P. *The Social Gospel of Walter Rauschenbusch and Its Relation to Religious Education*. New Haven: Yale University Press, 1944.

Brauer, Jerald C. *Protestantism in America*. Philadelphia: The Westminster Press, 1953.

Buckham, John W. *Progressive Religious Thought in America*. Boston: Houghton Mifflin Company, 1919.

Carter, Paul A. *The Decline and Revival of the Social Gospel*. New York: Cornell University Press, 1954.

Cauthen, Kenneth. *The Impact of American Religious Liberalism*. New York: Harper & Row, 1962.

Cavert, Samuel M., and Henry P. Dusen, editors. *The Church Through Half a Century*. New York: Charles Scribner's Sons, 1936.

Commager, Henry S. *The American Mind*. New York: Yale University Press, 1955.

Curtis, Susan. *A Consuming Faith: The Social Gospel and Modern American Culture*. Baltimore: The John Hopkins University Press, 1991.

Davies, D. R. *On to Orthodoxy*. London: Hodder and Stoughton, 1939.

DeWolf, L. Harold. *The Case for Theology in Liberal Perspective*. Philadelphia: The Westminster Press, 1959.

Dillenberger, John and Claude Welch. *Protestant Christianity Interpreted Through Its Development*. New York: Charles Scribner's Sons, 1954.

Dorrien, Gary J. *Reconstructing the Common Good: Theology and the Social Order*. Maryknoll NY: Orbis Books, 1990.

———. *The Making of American Liberal Theology: Idealism, Realism, & Modernity 1900–1950*. Louisville: Westminster/John Knox Press, 2003.

Douthat, Ross. *Bad Religion: How We Became a Nation of Heretics.* New York: Free Press, 2012.

Evans, Christopher H. *The Kingdom Is Always but Coming: A Life of Walter Rauschenbusch.* Grand Rapids MI: Eerdmans Publishing Co., 2004.

———, editor. *Perspectives on the Social Gospel.* Lewiston: Edwin Mellen Press, 1999.

———, editor. *The Social Gospel Today.* Louisville: Westminster/ John Knox Press, 2001.

Ferm, Vergilius, editor. *Encyclopedia of Religion.* Paterson: Littlefield, Adams and Company, 1959.

Fosdick, Harry Emerson. *The Living of These Days.* New York: Harper and Brothers, 1956.

Gabriel, Ralph H. *The Course of American Democratic Thought.* New York: The Ronald Press Company, 1940.

George, Timothy, and David S. Dockery, editors. *Baptist Theologians.* Nashville: Broadman Press, 1990.

Gladden, Washington. *Social Salvation.* Boston: Houghton Mifflin, 1902. Reprinted by Eugene OR: Wipf and Stock Publishers, 2004.

Haldeman, I. M. *Professor Rauschenbusch's Christianity and the Social Crisis.* New York: Charles C. Cook, 1911.

Hammar, George. *Christian Realism in Contemporary American Theology.* Upscala: A. B. Lundequistaka Bokhandeln, 1940.

Hershberger, Guy F., editor. *The Recovery of the Anabaptist Vision.* Scottdale: Herald Press, 1957.

Higgins, Paul L. *Preachers of Power.* New York: Vantage Press, Inc., 1950.

Hofmann, Hans. *The Theology of Reinhold Niebuhr.* Translated by Louise P. Smith. New York: Charles Scribner's Sons, 1956.

Hopkins, Charles H. *The Rise of the Social Gospel in American Protestantism, 1865–1915.* New Haven: Yale University Press, 1940.

Hordern, William. *A Layman's Guide to Protestant Theology.* New York: The Macmillan Company, 1960.

Horton, Walter Marshall. *Realistic Theology.* New York: Harper and Brothers, 1934.

Hudson, Winthrop. *The Great Tradition of the American Churches.* New York: Harper & Brothers, 1953.

Hughley, J. Neal. *Trends in Protestant Social Idealism.* New York: Kings Crown Press, 1948.

Hunt, George L., editor. *Ten Makers of Modern Protestant Thought.* New York: Association Press, 1958.

Johnson, F. Ernest. *The Social Gospel Re-Examined.* New York: Harper and Brothers, 1940.

Jones, E. Stanley. *Growing Spiritually.* New York: Abingdon Press, 1953.

Kegley, Charles W., and Robert W. Bretall, editors. *Reinhold Niebuhr, His Religious, Social, and Political Thought.* Volume 2 of the Library of Living Theology. New York: The Macmillan Company, 1956.

Kepler, Thomas S. *A Journey with the Saints.* Cleveland: The World Publishing Company, 1951.

Leonard, Bill J. *Baptists in America.* New York: Columbia University Press, 2005.

Lotz, Philip H., editor. *Founders of Christian Movements.* New York: Association Press, 1941.

McCown, Chester C. *The Genesis of the Social Gospel.* New York: Alfred A. Knopf, 1929.

McSwain, Larry L., and Wm. Loyd Allen, editors. *Twentieth-Century Shapers of Baptist Social Thought.* Macon GA: Mercer University Press, 2008.

Macfarlane, Charles, editor. *The Christian Ministry and the Social Order.* New Haven CT: Yale University Press, 1909.

Macquarrie, John. *Twentieth Century Religious Thought.* New York: Harper & Row, 1963.

Marsden, George M. *Fundamentalism and American Culture: The Shaping of Twentieth Century Evangelicalism, 1870–1925.* New York: Oxford University Press, 1980.

Marty, Martin E. *The Shape of American Religion.* New York: Harper and Brothers, 1959.

Mathews, Shailer, and G. B. Smith, editors. *A Dictionary of Religion and Ethics.* New York: The Macmillan Company, 1921.

Mattson, A. D. *Christian Social Consciousness.* Rock Island: Augustana Book Concern, 1953.

May, Henry F. *Protestant Churches and Industrial America.* New York: Harper and Brothers, 1949.

Meyer, Donald B. *The Protestant Search for Political Realism, 1919–1941.* Berkeley: University of California Press, 1961.

Minus, Paul M. *Walter Rauschenbusch: American Reformer.* New York: Macmillan Publishing Co., 1988.

Morrison, Charles C. *The Social Gospel and the Christian Cultus.* New York: Harper and Brothers, 1933.

Müller, Reinhart. *Walter Rauschenbusch.* Leiden: E. J. Brill, 1957.

Nash, Arnold S., editor. *Protestant Thought in the Twentieth Century.* New York: The Macmillan Company, 1951.

Niebuhr, H. Richard. *Christ and Culture.* New York: Harper and Brothers, 1951.

———. *The Kingdom of God in America.* New York: Harper and Brothers, 1937.

Niebuhr, Reinhold. *Faith and History.* New York: Charles Scribner's Sons, 1949.

———. *An Interpretation of Christian Ethics.* New York: Harper and Brothers, 1935.

———. *The Nature and Destiny of Man.* Volume 1. New York: Charles Scribner's Sons, 1949.

Osborn, Ronald E. *The Spirit of American Christianity.* New York: Harper and Brothers, 1958.

Ramsey, William M. *Four Modern Prophets: Walter Rauschenbusch, Martin Luther King, Jr., Gustavo Gutierrez, Rosemary Radford Ruether.* Atlanta: John Knox Press, 1986.

Roberts, David E., and Henry P. Van Dusen, editors. *Liberal Theology: An Appraisal.* New York: Charles Scribner's Sons, 1942.

Robertson, A. T. *The New Citizenship.* New York: Fleming H. Revell Company, 1919.

Rolston, Holmes. *The Social Message of the Apostle Paul.* Richmond: John Knox Press, 1942.

Ruether, Rosemary Radford. *The Radical Kingdom: The Western Experience of Messianic Hope.* New York: Harper & Row, Publishers, 1970.

Schleiermacher, Friedrich. *The Christian Faith*, edited and translated by H. R. Mackintosh and J. S. Stewart. Edinburgh: T. and T. Clark, 1928.

Sharpe, Dores Robinson. *Walter Rauschenbusch.* New York: The Macmillan Company, 1942.

Singer, Anna M. *Walter Rauschenbusch and His Contribution to Social Christianity.* Boston: Richard C. Badger, 1926.

Smith, Gerald B., editor. *Religious Thought in the Last Quarter-Century.* Chicago: The University of Chicago Press, 1927.

Smith, H. Shelton. *Changing Conceptions of Original Sin.* New York: Charles Scribner's Sons, 1955.

Smith, Timothy L. *Revivalism and Social Reform.* New York: Abingdon Press, 1957.

Smucker, Donovan E. *The Origins of Walter Rauschenbusch's Social Ethics.* Buffalo: McGill-Queen's University Press, 1994.

Sontag, Frederick, and John K. Roth. *The American Religious Experience: The Roots, Trends, and Future of Theology.* New York: Harper & Row, Publishers, 1972.

Sweet, Leonard. *Me and We: God's New Social Gospel.* Nashville: Abingdon, Press, 2014.

Tawney, R. H. *Religion and the Rise of Capitalism.* London: John Murray, 1948.

———. *Religion and the Rise of Capitalism.* London: John Murray, 1948.

Thelen, Mary Frances. *Man as Sinner in Contemporary American Realistic Theology.* Oxford: King Crown Press, 1946.

Thomas, George, F. *Christian Ethics and Moral Philosophy.* New York: Charles Scribner's Sons, 1955.

Thompson, Ernest T. *Changing Emphases in American Preaching.* Philadelphia: The Westminster Press, 1943.

Tillich, Paul. *Systematic Theology.* Volume 2. Chicago: The University of Chicago Press, 1957.

Torbet, Robert G. *The Baptist Ministry Then and Now.* Philadelphia: The Judson Press, 1953.

Tuck, William Powell. *Modern Shapers of Baptist Thought in America.* Richmond: Center for Baptist Heritage & Studies, 2012.

Tull, James E. *Shapers of Baptist Thought.* Valley Forge: Judson Press, 1972.

Visser't Hooft, W. A. *The Background of the Social Gospel in America.* Haarlem: H. D. Tjeenk Willink and Zoon, 1928.

Weisenburger, Francis P. *Ordeal of Faith: The Crisis of Church-Going America 1865–1900.* New York: Philosophical Library, 1959.

Whale, J. S. *Christian Doctrine.* Glasgow: Fontana Books, 1958.

White, Ronald C., and C. Howard Hopkins. *The Social Gospel: Religion and Reform in Changing America.* Philadelphia: Temple University Press, 1976.

2. Books: Parts of Series

Beard, Charles A., and Mary R. Beard. *The American Spirit*, vol. 4 of The Rise of American Civilization (4 vols). New York: The Macmillan Company, 1948.

Faulkner, H. U. *The Quest for Social Justice 1898–1914*, volume 11 of A History of American Life (12 volumes), edited by Arthur M. Schlesinger and D. R. Fox. New York: The Macmillan Company, 1931.

Schneider, Herbert W. *Religion in 20th Century America*, in The Library of Congress series in American Civilization, edited by Ralph H. Gabriel. Cambridge: Harvard University Press, 1952.

3. Periodicals

Altschuler, Glenn C. "Walter Rauschenbusch: Theology, the Church, and the Social Gospel." *Foundations* 22 (1997): 140–51.

Ashmall, Donald H. "Spiritual Development and the Free Church Tradition: The Inner Pilgrimage." *Andover-Newton Quarterly* 21 (January 1980): 141–52.

Bodein, Vernon P. "Walter Rauschenbusch." *Religion in Life* 6 (Summer 1937): 420–31.

Davis, Dennis R. "Impact of Evolutionary Thought on Walter Rauschenbusch." *Foundations* 38 (July–September 1978): 254–71.

Dickerson, Richard. "Rauschenbusch and Niebuhr: Brothers Under The Skin." *Religion in Life* 27 (Spring 1958): 163–71.

Evans, Christopher H. "Gender and the Kingdom of God: The Family Values of Walter Rauschenbusch." *American Baptist Quarterly* 19 (December 2000): 352–68.

———. "Ties That Bind: Walter Rauschenbusch, Reinhold Niebuhr and the Quest for Economic Justice." *Soundings* 95 (November 2012): 351–69.

Handy, Robert T. "The Protestant Quest for a Christian America." *Church History* 22 (March 1953): 8–20.

———. "Walter Rauschenbusch in Historical Perspective." *Baptist Quarterly* 20 (1964): 313–21.

Hopkins, Charles H. "Rauschenbusch and the Brotherhood of the Kingdom." *Church History* 7 (Winter 1938): 138–56.

Hudson, Winthrop S. "Rauschenbusch—Evangelical Prophet." *The Christian Century* 70 (24 June 1953): 740–42.

———. "Walter Rauschenbusch and the New Evangelism." *Religion and Life* 30 (1961): 412–30.

King, Martin Luther, Jr. "Pilgrimage to Nonviolence." *The Christian Century* 77 (13 April 1960): 439–41.

McGiffert, A. C., Jr. "Walter Rauschenbusch: Twenty Years After." *Christendom* 3 (Winter 1938): 98–109.

Marney, Carlyle. "The Significance of Walter Rauschenbusch for Today." *Foundations* 2 (January 1959): 13–26.

Massanari, Ronald Lee. "The Sacred Workshop of God: Reflections on the Historical Perspective of Walter Rauschenbusch." *Religion in Life* 39 (Summer 1971): 257–66.

Mathews, Shailer. "The Book of the Month." *The Biblical World* 41 (February 1913): 137–40.

Middleton, Robert G. "Social Christianity Yesterday and Today." *Religion in Life* 16 (Spring 1947): 186–97.

Moehlman, Conrad H. "The Life and Writings of Walter Rauschenbusch." *The Colgate-Rochester Divinity School Bulletin* 1 (October 1928): 32–37.

———. "Walter Rauschenbusch and His Interpreters." *Crozer Quarterly* 23 (January 1946): 34–50.

Morrison, C. C. "Is There a Social Gospel?" *The Christian Century* 61 (15 March 1944): 326–28.

———. "Orthodoxy, Too Has Its Social Gospel." *The Christian Century* 61 (1 March 1944): 262–64.

Mueller, William A. "The Life, Work and Gospel of Walter Rauschenbusch." *Religion in Life* 15 (Autumn 1946).

Niebuhr, Reinhold. "Walter Rauschenbusch in Historical Perspective." *Religion in Life* 27 (Autumn 1958): 527–36.

Niebuhr, H. Richard. "The Attack upon the Social Gospel." *Religion in Life* 5 (Spring 1936): 176–81.

Nixon, Justin W. "Walter Rauschenbusch after Forty Years." *Christendom* 12 (Autumn 1947): 476–85.

———. "Walter Rauschenbusch: The Man and His Work." *The Colgate-Rochester Divinity School Bulletin* 30 (May 1958): 21–32.

———. "The Social Philosophy of Walter Rauschenbusch." *The Colgate-Rochester Divinity School Bulletin* 1 (November 1928): 103–109.

Robins, Henry B. "The Contribution of Walter Rauschenbusch to World Peace." *The Colgate-Rochester Divinity School Bulletin* 12 (May 1940): 149–54.

———. "The Religion of Walter Rauschenbusch." *The Colgate-Rochester Divinity School Bulletin* 1 (October 1928): 37–43.

Rossol, Heinz D. "More than a Prophet." *American Baptist Quarterly* 29 (June 2000): 129–53.

Sanks, T. Holland. "Liberation Theology and the Social Gospel: Variations on a Theme." *Theological Studies* 40 (December 1980): 668–82.

Schneider, Carl E. "Americanization of Karl August Rauschenbusch, 1816–1899." *Church History* 24 (March 1955): 3–14.

Schroeder, John C. "A Deeper Social Gospel." *The Christian Century* 61 (26 July 1939): 922–25.

Sharpe, Dores R. "Walter Rauschenbusch—A Great Good Man." *The Colgate-Rochester Divinity School Bulletin* 12 (December 1939): 53–67.

Smucker, Donovan E. "Multiple Motifs in the Thought of Walter Rauschenbusch." *Encounter* 19 (Winter 1958): 14–20.

———. "Rauschenbusch after 50 Years." *The Christian Century* 74 (17 April 1957): 488–89.

———. "The Rauschenbusch Story." *Foundations* 2 (January 1959): 3–12.

———. "Walter Rauschenbusch: Anabaptist, Pietist, and Social Prophet." *Mennonite Life* 36 (1981): 21–23.

Stackhouse, Max L. "The Formation of a Prophet: Reflections on the Early Sermons of Walter Rauschenbusch." *Andover-Newton Quarterly* 9 (1969): 137–59.

Strain, Charles R. "Walter Rauschenbusch: A Resource for Public Theology." *Union Seminary Quarterly Review* 33 (Fall 1978): 23–24.

Visser't Hooft, W. A. "Rauschenbusch in Ecumenical Light," *The Colgate-Rochester Divinity School Bulletin* 30 (May 1958): 33–40.

Vulgamore, Melvin L. "The Social Gospel Old and New: Walter Rauschenbusch and Harvey Cox." *Religion in Life* 35 (Winter 1967): 516–33.

Ward, Harry F. "The Rauschenbusch Memorial." *Religious Education* 24 (April 1929): 297–98.

4. Encyclopedia Articles

Barnette, H. H. "Walter Rauschenbusch." *Encyclopedia of Southern Baptists*. Nashville: Broadman Press, 1958. 2:1133.

Crous, Ernest, and H. S. Bender. "Walter Rauschenbusch." *The Mennonite Encyclopedia*. Scottdale: Mennonite Publishing House, 1958. 4:256–257.

Evans, Christopher H. "Walter Rauschenbusch." *Dictionary of Modern American Philosophers*. Bristol, England: Thoemmes Press, 2005.

———. "Walter Rauschenbusch." *Encyclopedia of Christianity*, volume 4. Grand Rapids MI: Eerdmans, 2005.

Duff, E. "Walter Rauschenbusch." *New Catholic Encyclopedia*, second edition. 11, vol. Pau–Rd Detroit: Thomas Gale, 2003.

Fishburn, Janet F. "Walter Rauschenbusch 1861–1918." *The Encyclopedia of Protestantism*, volume L–R, edited by Hans J. Hillerbrand. New York: Routhledge, 2004.

Handy, R. T. "Walter Rauschenbusch." *Dictionary of Baptists in America*, edited by Bill L. Leonard. Downers Grove IL: InterVarsity Press, 1994. 231.

King, William McGuire. "Walter Rauschenbusch." *Concise Encyclopedia of Preaching*, edited by William H. Willimon and Richard Lischer. Louisville: Westminster/John Knox Press, 1995. 400–401.

Mathiasen, Elaine. "Walter Rauschenbusch." *Dictionary of World Biography: The 20th Century*, volume 9, O–Z. Pasadena: Salem Press, 1999. 3125–28.

Minus, Paul M. "Walter Rauschenbusch." *Encyclopedia of Religion*, second edition, edited by Lindsay Jones. Detroit: Thomas Gale, 2005.

Moehlman, Conrad Henry. "Walter Rauschenbusch." *Encyclopedia of Religion*, edited by Vergilius Ferm. Paterson NJ: Littlefield, Adams & Co., 1959. 635.

Vernon, Ambrose White. "Later Theology." *The Cambridge History of American Literature*. New York: The Macmillan Company, 1936. 3:215.

"Walter Rauschenbusch." *American National Biography*, edited by John A. Garraty and Mark C. Carnes, volume 18. New York: Oxford University Press, 1995.

"Walter Rauschenbusch 1861–1918." *Historical Dictionary of the Baptists*, second edition, edited by William H. Brackney. Lanham MD: The Scarecrow Press, Inc., 2009.

"Walter Rauschenbusch." *The Columbia Encyclopedia*, second edition. New York: Columbia University Press, 1950. 1644.

"Walter Rauschenbusch." *The Encyclopedia Americana* New York: Americana Corporation, 1959. 23:232.

"Walter Rauschenbusch 1861–1918." *The Mennonite Encyclopedia*, volume 4, O–Z, edited by Harold S. Bender and C. Henry Smith. Scottdale PA: The Mennonite Publishing House, 1959.

"Walter Rauschenbusch." *The New International Encyclopedia*, second edition. New York: Dodd, Mead, and Company, 1916. 19:569–70.

"Walter Rauschenbusch." *Who's Who in America 1918–19.* New York: The Macmillan Company, 1919. 9:2022.

Ward, Harry F. "Walter Rauschenbusch." *Dictionary of American Biography.* New York: Charles Scribner's Sons, 1935.

5. Unpublished Materials

Allen, Jimmy Raymond. "Comparative Study of the Concept of the Kingdom of God in the Writings of Walter Rauschenbusch and Reinhold Niebuhr." Unpublished Doctor of Theology dissertation. Southwestern Baptist Theological Seminary, 1958.

Barnette, H. H. "The Ethical Thought of Walter Rauschenbusch: A Critical Interpretation." Unpublished Doctor of Theology thesis. The Southern Baptist Theological Seminary, Louisville KY, 1948.

Battenhouse, Paul F. "Theology in the Social Gospel, 1918–1946." Unpublished Doctor of Philosophy dissertation. Yale University, 1950.

Bond, Richard Ellison, Jr. "A Critical Analysis of the Concept of Justice in Paul Tillich, Heinrich Rommen, and Walter Rauschenbusch." Unpublished Doctor of Philosophy dissertation. Yale University, 1972.

Brunson, Drexel Timothy. "The Quest for Social Justice: A Study of Walter Rauschenbusch and His Influence on Reinhold Niebuhr and Martin Luther King, Jr." Unpublished Doctor of Philosophy dissertation. Florida State University, December 1980.

Burckhardt, Abel E. "Walter Rauschenbusch as a Representative of American Humanism." Unpublished Th.M. thesis. Union Theological Seminary, 1925.

Dale, Verhey Allen, "The Use of Scripture in Moral Discourse: A Case Study of Walter Rauschenbusch." Unpublished Doctor of Philosophy dissertation. Yale University, 1975.

David, William E. "A Comparative Study of the Social Ethics of Walter Rauschenbusch and Reinhold Niebuhr." Unpublished Doctor of Philosophy dissertation. Vanderbilt University, 1958.

Fricke, Ernest E. "Socialism in Christianity in Walter Rauschenbusch." Unpublished Doctor of Theology dissertation. University of Basel, 1965.

Harry, David Roy. "Two Kingdoms: Walter Rauschenbusch's Concept of the Kingdom of God Contrasted with the Theology of Revivalism in Early Twentieth Century America." Unpublished Doctor of Philosophy dissertation. Southwestern Baptist Theological Seminary, 1993.

Hordern, William E., "The Theology of the Social Gospel," unpublished Master of Theology thesis. Union Theological Seminary, New York, 1946.

Horne, Cleveland R., Jr. "Christian Economic Ethics: A Study of Contemporary Thought in the Light of the Works of Walter Rauschenbusch." Unpublished Doctor of Philosophy dissertation. Southwestern Baptist Theological Seminary, 1956.

Horton, Natalie R. "The Life, Work and Influence of Walter Rauschenbusch." Unpublished Master's thesis. American Baptist Theological Seminary, 1951.

Johnson, Carl Ebert. "Walter Rauschenbusch as Historian." Unpublished Doctor of Philosophy dissertation. Duke University, 1976.

Knouse, Frank E. "The Concept of the Kingdom of God in the Thought and Work of Walter Rauschenbusch." Unpublished Master of Theology thesis. University of Southern California, Los Angeles, 1948.

Locke, Harvey James. "Rauschenbusch." Unpublished Doctor of Philosophy dissertation. University of Chicago, 1930.

McClintock, David Alan. "Walter Rauschenbusch: The Kingdom of God and the American Experience." Unpublished Doctor of Philosophy dissertation. Case Western Reserve University, 1975.

Magill, Sherry Patricia. "The Political Thought of Walter Rauschenbusch: Toward a Religious Theory of the Positive State."

Unpublished Doctor of Philosophy dissertation. Syracuse University, 1984.

McInerny, William Francis, Jr. "Scripture and Christian Ethics: An Evaluative Analysis of the Use of Scripture in the Works of Walter Rauschenbusch." Unpublished Doctor of Philosophy dissertation. Marquette University, 1984.

McNab, John Ingram. "Towards a Theology of Social Concern: A Comparative Study in the Elements for Social Concern in the Writings of Frederick D. Maurice and Walter Rauschenbusch." Unpublished Doctor of Philosophy dissertation. McGill University, 1972.

Merriwether, David Peck. "An Exercise in Ethical Method: An Analysis of the Ethics of Walter Rauschenbusch with Reference to his Views on Economic Morality." Unpublished Doctor of Philosophy dissertation. Duke University, 1986.

Norment, Owen Lennon, Jr. "A Study of the Social Ethics of Walter Rauschenbusch and Reinhold Niebuhr." Unpublished Master of Theology thesis. Union Theological Seminary, Richmond VA, May 1959.

Rossol, Heinz D. "Walter Rauschenbusch as Preacher: The Development of His Social Thought as Expressed in His Sermons from 1886–1897." Unpublished Doctor of Philosophy dissertation. Marquette University, 1997.

Schirmer, Carolyn Best. "Theological Method in Walter Rauschenbusch: An Analysis and Critique of His Use of the Bible." Unpublished Master's thesis. The American University, 1968.

Smucker, Donovan E. "The Origins of Walter Rauschenbusch's Social Ethics." Unpublished Doctor of Philosophy thesis. University of Chicago, Chicago, 1957 (later published in 1994).

Stackhouse, Max, "Eschatology and Ethical Method: A Structural Analysis of Contemporary Christian Social Ethics in America with Primary Reference to Walter Rauschenbusch and Reinhold Niebuhr." Unpublished Doctor of Philosophy dissertation. Harvard University, 1965.

Trench, William Crowell. "The Social Gospel and the City: Implications for Theological Reconstruction in the Work of Washington Gladden, Josiah Strong, and Walter Rauschenbusch." Unpublished Doctor of Philosophy dissertation. Boston University, 1986.

True, David Bryan. "Faithful Politics: The Traditions of Martin Luther King, Jr., Reinhold Niebuhr, and Walter Rauschenbusch." Unpublished Doctor of Philosophy dissertation. Union Theological Seminary and Presbyterian School of Christian Education, Richmond VA, December 2005.

Tuck, William Powell. "The Concept of Soteriology in the Theology of Walter Rauschenbusch." Unpublished Master of Theology thesis. Southeastern Baptist Theological Seminary, Wake Forest NC, April 1961.

Verhey, Allen Dale. "The Use of Scripture in Moral Discourse: A Case Study of Walter Rauschenbusch." Unpublished Doctor of Philosophy dissertation. Yale University, 1975.

Weatherly, Owen. "A Comparative Study of the Social Ethics of Walter Rauschenbusch and Reinhold Niebuhr." Unpublished Master's thesis. University of Chicago, 1950.

Williams, Claude J. "Walter Rauschenbusch: A Prophet for Social Righteousness." Unpublished Doctor of Philosophy dissertation. Southern Baptist Theological Seminary, 1952.

Index

Adam 51–53

Anti-Catholicism 132

Aquinas, Thomas 47, 62

Asceticism 9, 69, 82–83, 86, 126

Atonement 3, 5–6, 8–9, 14, 35, 69, 71, 91, 96–97, 100–102, 115, 128

Atonement and racial solidarity 9, 91, 96

Augustine 47

Barbour, Clarence A. 30

Barclay, William 90

Barnes, L. C. 77

Beach, Waldo 46, 116

Beecher, Henry Ward 16, 22

Bell, Rob 90

Bellamy, Edward 18, 30

Bennett, John C. 63, 133, 136

Biblical criticism 20, 51

Bodein, Vernon P. 9, 54, 65

Bonhoeffer, Dietrich 25

Booth, William 108

Branchlow, Stephen 25

Broadus, John A. 30

Brooks, Philip 16

Brotherhood of the Kingdom 19, 31–32, 37, 41, 149

Brown, Robert McAfee 133, 136

Brown, William Adams 26, 63, 108

Brunson, Drexel Timothy 111, 120, 154

Bunyan, John 14

Bushnell, Horace 25, 97

Calvin, John 15, 47, 108

Campolo, Tony 71, 87

Cauthen, Kenneth 23, 26, 39

Chittister, Joan 111, 120

Christ xiv, 6–8, 18, 20, 43, 50, 52–53, 56, 59, 71–72, 74–76, 78, 83, 92, 94, 96–97, 99–103, 106–10, 115–16, 125, 127, 134–35, 146

Christian socialist 29, 132

Christianity and the Social Crisis xv, 2, 9–10, 34, 40, 65–66, 87–90, 95, 116–20, 139, 142, 144

Christianizing the Social Order xv, 9, 18, 22, 35, 40, 60, 65–67, 88–89, 117–19, 139

Church as the social factor in redemption 5, 9, 91, 108, 133

Class contempt 98, 128

Coffin, Henry Sloane 114, 120

Colgate-Rochester Divinity School Bulletin 37, 150–52

Collective sin 5, 8, 44, 58, 125

Communist Manifesto 17–18

Cox, Harvey 26, 39, 152

Dare We Be Christians? 137, 139

Death vi, xiii, 3, 36–37, 46, 50–51, 72, 76, 83–84, 90–91, 96–102, 126, 128, 135

of Christ/Jesus 96–101, 128

Devil 33, 44, 49, 61–62, 125

Dickerson, Richard 48, 64

Dillenberger, John 10, 14, 21, 38

Dorrien, Gary 4, 39, 43, 131

Douthat, Ross 104, 118

Drummond, Henry 30

Dusen, Henry P. Van 21, 23, 25, 119, 147

Edwards, Jonathan 25

Ely, Richard T. 18

Emerson, Ralph Waldo 25

Equality of women 133

Eschatology 35, 85, 133–34, 136, 156

Evangelical xi, 25, 77, 87, 142, 150

Existentialist philosophy 6

Experiential religion 76

Evans, Christopher H. 2, 9–10, 22, 38–39, 116, 119, 121, 136

Faith i, xi, xiii–xiv, 22–23, 35, 39, 41, 64, 66, 70–72, 74–76, 79–80, 83–84, 86, 91–92, 104–105, 110, 114–16, 118, 126–27, 129–30, 134–35, 143, 146–48

Fant, Clyde E. Jr., 11

Federal Council of the Churches of Christ 20

Ferré, Nels F. S. 90

For the Right 31, 40, 73

Fosdick, Harry Emerson 26, 37, 42, 131, 136

Fundamentalism 95, 117, 146

George, Henry 29–30

George, Timothy 10, 38

Gilman, Paine 30

Gladden, Washington 18, 22, 114, 120, 157

Gomes, Peter 20

Graft 53, 98, 128

Haldeman, I. M. 94, 117

Hale, Edward Everett 19

Hammar, George 48, 64

Handy, Robert T. 9, 22, 40, 47, 136

Hasting, Robert 30

Hauerwas, Stanley 2, 10, 105, 119

Heath, Richard 30

INDEX

Hell's Kitchen xi, 28, 30, 123–24

Holmes, John Haynes 37, 131

Hooft, W. A. Visser't 10, 23

Hopkins, C. H. 9–10, 21–23, 39–40, 120, 143–44, 148–49

Hordern, William E. 55, 66

Hubris 47

Hudson, Winthrop S. 9–10, 121

Human awareness of sin 44

Humanism 154

Immortality 9, 69, 83–84

In His Steps xiii, 19

James, William 25

Jesus i, vi, xiii–xiv, 3, 6, 9, 14, 19, 21, 23, 26–27, 30–31, 33–35, 41, 50–53, 58, 66–67, 69–71, 75–79, 82–83, 87–88, 91–92, 94–102, 106, 108–11, 113, 115–16, 118–20, 128–30, 133, 140

Johnson, F. Ernest 118

Jones, E. Stanley 85, 90

Judson, Edward 30

Kagawa 37, 131

King, Henry C. 71

King, Martin Luther Jr. 3, 11, 25, 37–39, 42, 107, 118, 120, 131, 133, 136, 147, 154, 157

King, William 26

Kingdom of Evil 5, 7–8, 36, 44, 56, 58, 60–62, 79, 84, 87, 97, 100, 102, 107–108, 113, 115, 124–25, 127, 130, 132, 134

Kingdom of God xiii–xv, 3, 6–7, 14, 17, 31–32, 34–36, 45, 50, 56, 58, 63, 72, 78–79, 82, 84, 86–87, 91–93, 100–102, 104–105, 108, 110–16, 118, 124–25, 129–30, 132–34, 146, 149, 154–55

Land, Richard 21, 23

Landis, Benson Y. 9, 39, 90, 117

Left Behind vi, 78

Leonard, Bill J. 22, 65

Lewis, Paul 2, 10, 26, 39

Liberalism 23, 26, 39, 143

Liberation theology 26, 133, 151

Lincoln, Abraham 25

Luther, Martin 47

MacLaren, Alexander 30

Marsden, George 95

Marshall, Molly T. 90

Marty, Martin E. 119

Marxism 17

Marxist socialism 17

Mathews, Shailer 19, 21, 69, 87, 140

Maurice, F. D. 18, 30

Mazzini, Giuseppe 30

McConnell, Francis J. 37, 131

Melville, Herman 25

Merrick Lectures 34

Meyer, Donald 77

Meyer, F. W. C. 29, 40

Militarism 98, 128

Mill, J. S. 30

Minus, Paul M. 9–10, 38

Moehlmann, Conrad Henry 36

Moltmann, Jurgen 90

Moody, D. L. 30, 90

Mysticism 9, 69, 81–82, 86, 126–27, 129

Nathaniel W. Taylor Lectures 35

National Council of Churches 131

Nature of Sin 4–5, 8, 44, 46, 49–50, 53–55, 57–58, 78–79, 93, 124–25

Neue Lieder 77, 139

New Evangelism 116, 121, 140, 150

Niebuhr, H. Richard 43, 63, 102, 116, 118, 141

Niebuhr, Reinhold 11, 25, 38, 47, 64, 74, 88, 118, 120, 131, 136, 142, 144–45, 149, 154–57

Nixon, Justin Wroe 37, 42

Northern Baptist Convention 108

Orthodoxy 3, 14, 62, 80, 143, 150

Original sin, 4–5, 8, 44, 50–51, 53–56, 59, 64, 93, 104, 124, 147

Osgood, Howard 28

Ottati, Douglas 29

Oxnam, G. Bromley 4, 11

Pascal 47, 64

Paul 52, 59, 75, 82, 87, 102

Peitz, Darlene Ann 4, 11, 89

Porter, R. E. 19

Prayers of the Social Awakening xv, 2, 9, 34, 39, 58, 66, 116, 119, 136–37, 140

Premillennialism 95

Prophetic religion 101, 115, 128

Puritan theology 19, 23, 123

Racial solidarity 4–5, 7, 9, 54, 91, 96, 102, 115, 128

Ramsay, William M. 26, 131, 147

Ransom 97

Rauschenbusch, August 27, 39, 139, 151

Raushenbush, Paul 2, 10, 71

Raymond, J. E. 30

Reconciliation 97, 100

Redemption ix, xiii–xiv, 1, 5–6, 8–9, 21, 27, 31, 43, 50, 56, 60, 71–72, 77, 79, 86, 91, 93–95, 97, 99, 101–109, 111–13, 115, 117, 119, 121, 124–26, 129–30, 133–34

    of the super-personal entities 103

    personal 8, 21, 71, 86, 91, 125–26, 130, 134

    social ix, 5, 8–9, 71, 77, 91, 93–95, 97, 99, 101–104, 105, 107, 109, 111, 113, 115, 116–17, 119, 121, 129

Reformation xiv, 25, 37, 62, 73–75, 93, 107–109

Religious bigotry 98, 128

Revivalism 14, 20, 23, 123, 147, 155

Righteousness xiv–xv, 1–2, 9–11, 38, 50, 55, 59, 72, 88, 91, 101, 104, 112–13, 116, 119–20, 127, 140–41, 157

Righteousness of the Kingdom, The xiv–xv, 9, 11, 38, 72, 88, 91, 116, 119–20, 140–41

Riis, Jacob 30

Riley, William B. 36

Ritschl, Albrecht 30, 66

Robertson, A. T. 71, 87

Robins, Henry B. 33

Rochester Theological Seminary 27–28, 33, 36, 38, 40–42, 65, 88–89, 118, 141–42

Rorty, Richard 78, 89

Ross, E. A. 30

Rother, Pauline 32

Royce, Josiah 30, 59, 67

Ruether, Rosemary Radford 39, 118, 120, 147

Ruskin, John 30

Ryan, John 74, 132

Sacredness of personality 69–70

Salvation i–v, ix, xi, xiv–xv, 1, 3–9, 14, 35, 43–44, 49, 60, 69, 71–72, 74–87, 90–97, 101, 103, 108, 110–12, 114–15, 120, 123, 125–27, 129–30, 133–34, 143–44

  personal i, ix, 5, 7–8, 69, 71, 77, 80–81, 86, 123, 125–26, 129

  social xv, 71, 91, 114, 120, 143–44

Satanology 4–5, 8, 44, 61

Schleiermacher, Fredrich 30, 55, 58, 66, 110, 147

Sermon on the Mount 70

Sharpe, Dores Robinson 9, 23, 38, 65, 88, 136

Sheldon, Charles xiii

Shriver, Donald 2

Sin i–ii, ix, xiv, 4–8, 35, 43–51, 53–61, 63–65, 67, 72, 76, 78–79, 82, 84, 92–104, 112, 115, 123–28, 130, 134, 147

  as selfishness 48, 78, 94

  original 4–5, 8, 44, 50–51, 53–56, 59, 64, 93, 104, 124, 147

  personal i, 5, 8, 44, 56, 124

  social i

Singer, Anna M. 120

Smith, Adam 16

Smith, H. Shelton 49, 64

Smucker Donovan E. 134, 136, 141

Social Darwinism 104

Social gospel i–ii, ix, xi, xiv–xv, 1–6, 8–10, 13–23, 25–26, 32, 34–37, 39–44, 46, 49–50, 53, 56–57, 59–61, 63–67, 77, 81, 84, 88–90, 92–93, 95–96, 100–102, 104–105, 107–108, 111, 114, 116–21, 123–25, 129, 133, 136, 140–41, 143–52, 154–55, 157

Social gospel movement ix, xi, 13–15, 17, 19, 21–23, 34, 114, 123, 133

Social gospel novel 19

Social implications of salvation 9, 91, 96, 130

Social justice xi, 23, 84, 102, 119–20, 149, 154

Social Principles of Jesus 9, 35, 41, 66–67, 69, 87–88, 102, 116, 118–20, 140

Social problems 13, 18–19, 22, 29–30, 35, 114, 123

Socialism 17, 29, 31, 104, 107, 140, 155

Socialist xi, 18, 29, 132

Solidaristic comprehension 5, 69, 78, 81, 94, 96

Solidarity of humanity 4, 61, 79, 125

Soteriology 4–7, 63, 69, 91, 157

Sovereignty of God 47, 133

Specific economic remedies 132

Stackhouse, Max xv, 3, 20, 25, 40, 132

Stake of the church in the social movement 141

Strong, Josiah 18, 34, 157

Super-personal entities 5, 7–9, 60, 91, 102–103, 115, 127

Tawney, R. H. 15, 22

Taylor, Graham 30

Taylor, J. Hudson 30

Thelen, Mary Frances 43, 63

Theology for the Social Gospel, A xv, 9–10, 19, 21, 35, 37, 42, 63–67, 81, 88–90, 92, 116–20, 140

Tillich, Paul 47, 64, 154

Tolstoy, Leo 30

Torbet, Robert G. 148

Transcendence of God 6, 93

True, David Bryan 11, 118

Tuck, William Powell i, iv–vi, 10, 90

Tull, James E. 1, 10, 148

Unto Me 9, 35, 89, 116, 140

Waldo, Peter 108

Warren, Rick 71

Weaver, Douglas 71, 87

Welch, Claude 10, 14, 21, 38, 143

Wesley, John 108

Whale, J. S. 80, 89

White, Ronald C. Jr., 10, 22

"Why I Am a Baptist" 76, 88, 141

Williams, Leighton 30–31

Willimon, William H. 10, 39, 90, 153

World War I xi, 36, 114, 131

Wright, N. T. 90

Wycliffe, John 108

Zwingli, Hulderich 108–109

Other available titles from

#Connect
Reaching Youth Across the Digital Divide
Brian Foreman

Reaching our youth across the digital divide is a struggle for parents, ministers, and other adults who work with Generation Z—today's teenagers. #*Connect* leads readers into the technological landscape, encourages conversations with teenagers, and reminds us all to be the presence of Christ in every facet of our lives.   978-1-57312-693-9 *120 pages/pb* **$13.00**

Beginnings
A Reverend and a Rabbi Talk About the Stories of Genesis
Michael Smith and Rami Shapiro

Editor Aaron Herschel Shapiro declares that stories "must be retold—not just repeated, but reinvented, reimagined, and reexperienced" to remain vital in the world. Mike and Rami continue their conversations from the *Mount and Mountain* books, exploring the places where their traditions intersect and diverge, listening to each other as they respond to the stories of Genesis.   978-1-57312-772-1 *202 pages/pb* **$18.00**

Choosing Gratitude
Learning to Love the Life You Have
James A. Autry

Autry reminds us that gratitude is a choice, a spiritual—not social—process. He suggests that if we cultivate gratitude as a way of being, we may not change the world and its ills, but we can change our response to the world. If we fill our lives with moments of gratitude, we will indeed love the life we have.   978-1-57312-614-4 *144 pages/pb* **$15.00**

Choosing Gratitude 365 Days a Year
Your Daily Guide to Grateful Living
James A. Autry and Sally J. Pederson

Filled with quotes, poems, and the inspired voices of both Pederson and Autry, in a society consumed by fears of not having "enough"—money, possessions, security, and so on—this book suggests that if we cultivate gratitude as a way of being, we may not change the world and its ills, but we can change our response to the world.   978-1-57312-689-2 *210 pages/pb* **$18.00**

To order call **1-800-747-3016** or visit **www.helwys.com**

Crossroads in Christian Growth
W. Loyd Allen

Authentic Christian life presents spiritual crises and we struggle to find a hero walking with God at a crossroads. With wisdom and sincerity, W. Loyd Allen presents Jesus as our example and these crises as stages in the journey of growth we each take toward maturity in Christ.
978-1-57312-753-0 164 pages/pb **$15.00**

A Divine Duet
Ministry and Motherhood
Alicia Davis Porterfield, ed.

Each essay in this inspiring collection is as different as the mother-minister who wrote it, from theologians to chaplains, inner-city ministers to rural-poverty ministers, youth pastors to preachers, mothers who have adopted, birthed, and done both.
978-1-57312-676-2 146 pages/pb **$16.00**

The Exile and Beyond (All the Bible series)
Wayne Ballard

The Exile and Beyond brings to life the sacred literature of Israel and Judah that comprises the exilic and postexilic communities of faith. It covers Ezekiel, Isaiah, Haggai, Zechariah, Malachi, 1 & 2 Chronicles, Ezra, Nehemiah, Joel, Jonah, Song of Songs, Esther, and Daniel.
978-1-57312-759-2 196 pages/pb **$16.00**

Ezekiel (Smyth & Helwys Annual Bible Study series)
God's Presence in Performance
William D. Shiell

Through a four-session Bible study for individuals and groups, Shiell interprets the book of Ezekiel as a four-act drama to be told to those living out their faith in a strange, new place. Shiell encourages congregations to listen to God's call, accept where God has planted them, surrender the shame of their past, receive a new heart from God, and allow God to breathe new life into them.
Teaching Guide 978-1-57312-755-4 192 pages/pb **$14.00**
Study Guide 978-1-57312-756-1 126 pages/pb **$6.00**

Fierce Love
Desperate Measures for Desperate Times
Jeanie Miley

Fierce Love is about learning to see yourself and know yourself as a conduit of love, operating from a full heart instead of trying to find someone to whom you can hook up your emotional hose and fill up your empty heart.
978-1-57312-810-0 276 pages/pb **$18.00**

To order call **1-800-747-3016** or visit **www.helwys.com**

Five Hundred Miles
Reflections on Calling and Pilgrimage
Lauren Brewer Bass

Spain's Camino de Santiago, the Way of St. James, has been a cherished pilgrimage path for centuries, visited by countless people searching for healing, solace, purpose, and hope. These stories from her five-hundred-mile-walk is Lauren Brewer Bass's honest look at the often winding, always surprising journey of a calling. 978-1-57312-812-4 142 pages/pb **$16.00**

Galatians (Smyth & Helwys Bible Commentary)
Marion L. Soards and Darrell J. Pursiful

In Galatians, Paul endeavored to prevent the Gentile converts from embracing a version of the gospel that insisted on their observance of a form of the Mosaic Law. He saw with a unique clarity that such a message reduced the crucified Christ to being a mere agent of the Law. For Paul, the gospel of Jesus Christ alone, and him crucified, had no place in it for the claim that Law-observance was necessary for believers to experience the power of God's grace. 978-1-57312-771-4 384 pages/hc **$55.00**

God's Servants the Prophets
Bryan Bibb

God's Servants, the Prophets covers the Israelite and Judean prophetic literature from the preexilic period. It includes Amos, Hosea, Isaiah, Micah, Zephaniah, Nahum, Habakkuk, Jeremiah, and Obadiah.
978-1-57312-758-5 208 pages/pb **$16.00**

Hermeneutics of Hymnody
A Comprehensive and Integrated Approach to Understanding Hymns
Scotty Gray

Scotty Gray's *Hermeneutics of Hymnody* is a comprehensive and integrated approach to understanding hymns. It is unique in its holistic and interrelated exploration of seven of the broad facets of this most basic forms of Christian literature. A chapter is devoted to each and relates that facet to all of the others. 978-157312-767-7 432 pages/pb **$28.00**

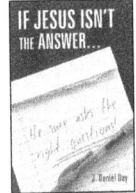

If Jesus Isn't the Answer . . . He Sure Asks the Right Questions!
J. Daniel Day

Taking eleven of Jesus' questions as its core, Day invites readers into their own conversation with Jesus. Equal parts testimony, theological instruction, pastoral counseling, and autobiography, the book is ultimately an invitation to honest Christian discipleship.
978-1-57312-797-4 148 pages/pb **$16.00**

To order call 1-800-747-3016 or visit www.helwys.com

I'm Trying to Lead . . . Is Anybody Following?
The Challenge of Congregational Leadership in the Postmodern World
Charles B. Bugg

Bugg provides us with a view of leadership that has theological integrity, honors the diversity of church members, and reinforces the brave hearts of church leaders who offer vision and take risks in the service of Christ and the church.
978-1-57312-731-8 136 pages/pb **$13.00**

James M. Dunn and Soul Freedom
Aaron Douglas Weaver

James Milton Dunn, over the last fifty years, has been the most aggressive Baptist proponent for religious liberty in the US. Soul freedom—voluntary, uncoerced faith and an unfettered individual conscience before God—is the basis of his understanding of church-state separation and the historic Baptist basis of religious liberty.
978-1-57312-590-1 224 pages/pb **$18.00**

The Jesus Tribe
Following Christ in the Land of the Empire
Ronnie McBrayer

The Jesus Tribe fleshes out the implications, possibilities, contradictions, and complexities of what it means to live within the Jesus Tribe and in the shadow of the American Empire.
978-1-57312-592-5 208 pages/pb **$17.00**

Judaism
A Brief Guide to Faith and Practice
Sharon Pace

Sharon Pace's newest book is a sensitive and comprehensive introduction to Judaism. How does belief in the One God and a universal morality shape the way in which Jews see the world? How does one find meaning in life and the courage to endure suffering? How does one mark joy and forge community ties?
978-1-57312-644-1 144 pages/pb **$16.00**

Looking Around for God
The Strangely Reverent Observations of an Unconventional Christian
James A. Autry

Looking Around for God, Autry's tenth book, is in many ways his most personal. In it he considers his unique life of faith and belief in God. Autry is a former Fortune 500 executive, author, poet, and consultant whose work has had a significant influence on leadership thinking.
978-157312-484-3 144 pages/pb **$16.00**

To order call 1-800-747-3016 or visit www.helwys.com

Marriage Ministry: A Guidebook
Bo Prosser and Charles Qualls

This book is equally helpful for ministers, for nearly/newlywed couples, and for thousands of couples across our land looking for fresh air in their marriages. 1-57312-432-X 160 pages/pb **$16.00**

Meeting Jesus Today
For the Cautious, the Curious, and the Committed
Jeanie Miley

Meeting Jesus Today, ideal for both individual study and small groups, is intended to be used as a workbook. It is designed to move readers from studying the Scriptures and ideas within the chapters to recording their journey with the Living Christ.

978-1-57312-677-9 320 pages/pb **$19.00**

The Ministry Life
101 Tips for Ministers' Spouses
John and Anne Killinger

While no pastor does his or her work alone, roles for a spouse or partner are much more flexible and fluid now than they once were. Spouses who want to support their minister-mates' vocation may wonder where to begin. Whatever your talents may be, the Killingers have identified a way to put those gifts to work. 978-1-57312-769-1 252 pages/pb **$19.00**

The Ministry Life
101 Tips for New Ministers
John Killinger

Sharing years of wisdom from more than fifty years in ministry and teaching, The Ministry Life: 101 Tips for New Ministers by John Killinger is filled with practical advice and wisdom for a minister's day-to-day tasks as well as advice on intellectual and spiritual habits to keep ministers of any age healthy and fulfilled. 978-1-57312-662-5 244 pages/pb **$19.00**

Mount and Mountain
Vol. 2: A Reverend and a Rabbi Talk About the Sermon on the Mount
Rami Shapiro and Michael Smith

This book, focused on the Sermon on the Mount, represents the second half of Mike and Rami's dialogue. In it, Mike and Rami explore the text of Jesus' sermon cooperatively, contributing perspectives drawn from their lives and religious traditions and seeking moments of illumination. 978-1-57312-654-0 254 pages/pb **$19.00**

To order call 1-800-747-3016 or visit www.helwys.com

Of Mice and Ministers
Musings and Conversations About Life, Death, Grace, and Everything
Bert Montgomery

With stories about pains, joys, and everyday life, Of Mice and Ministers finds Jesus in some unlikely places and challenges us to do the same. From tattooed women ministers to saying the "N"-word to the brotherly kiss, Bert Montgomery takes seriously the lesson from Psalm 139—where can one go that God is not already there?   978-1-57312-733-2 154 pages/pb **$14.00**

Place Value
The Journey to Where You Are
Katie Sciba

Does a place have value? Can a place change us? Is it possible for God to use the place you are in to form you? From Victoria, Texas to Indonesia, Belize, Australia, and beyond, Katie Sciba's wanderlust serves as a framework to understand your own places of deep emotion and how God may have been weaving redemption around you all along.

978-157312-829-2 138 pages/pb **$15.00**

Preacher Breath
Sermon & Essays
Kyndall Rae Rothaus

"*Preacher Breath* is a worthy guide, leading the reader room by room with wisdom, depth, and a spiritual maturity far beyond her years, so that the preaching house becomes a holy, joyful home. . . . This book is soul kindle for a preacher's heart."   —Danielle Shroyer
Pastor, Author of *The Boundary-Breaking God*

978-1-57312-734-9 208 pages/pb **$16.00**

Quiet Faith
An Introvert's Guide to Spiritual Survival
Judson Edwards

In eight finely crafted chapters, Edwards looks at key issues like evangelism, interpreting the Bible, dealing with doubt, and surviving the church from the perspective of a confirmed, but sometimes reluctant, introvert. In the process, he offers some provocative insights that introverts will find helpful and reassuring.   978-1-57312-681-6 144 pages/pb **$15.00**

To order call **1-800-747-3016** or visit **www.helwys.com**

Reading Deuteronomy
(Reading the Old Testament series)
A Literary and Theological Commentary
Stephen L. Cook

A lost treasure for large segments of today's world, the book of Deuteronomy stirs deep longing for God and moves readers to a place of intimacy with divine otherness, holism, and will for person-centered community. The consistently theological interpretation reveals the centrality of this book for faith.
978-1-57312-757-8 286 pages/pb **$22.00**

Reflective Faith
A Theological Toolbox for Women
Susan M. Shaw

In *Reflective Faith*, Susan Shaw offers a set of tools to explore difficult issues of biblical interpretation, theology, church history, and ethics—especially as they relate to women. Reflective faith invites intellectual struggle and embraces the unknown; it is a way of discipleship, a way to love God with your mind, as well as your heart, your soul, and your strength.
978-1-57312-719-6 292 pages/pb **$24.00**
Workbook 978-1-57312-754-7 164 pages/pb **$12.00**

Sessions with Psalms (Sessions Bible Studies series)
Prayers for All Seasons
Eric and Alicia D. Porterfield

Useful to seminar leaders during preparation and group discussion, as well as in individual Bible study, *Sessions with Psalms* is a ten-session study designed to explore what it looks like for the words of the psalms to become the words of our prayers. Each session is followed by a thought-provoking page of questions.
978-1-57312-768-4 136 pages/pb **$14.00**

Sessions with Revelation
(Sessions Bible Studies series)
The Final Days of Evil
David Sapp

David Sapp's careful guide through Revelation demonstrates that it is a letter of hope for believers; it is less about the last days of history than it is about the last days of evil. Without eliminating its mystery, Sapp unlocks Revelation's central truths so that its relevance becomes clear.
978-1-57312-706-6 166 pages/pb **$14.00**

To order call 1-800-747-3016 or visit www.helwys.com

Though the Darkness Gather Round
Devotions about Infertility, Miscarriage, and Infant Loss

Mary Elizabeth Hill Hanchey and Erin McClain, eds.

Much courage is required to weather the long grief of infertility and the sudden grief of miscarriage and infant loss. This collection of devotions by men and women, ministers, chaplains, and lay leaders who can speak of such sorrow, is a much-needed resource and precious gift for families on this journey and the faith communities that walk beside them.

978-1-57312-811-7 180 pages/pb **$19.00**

Time for Supper
Invitations to Christ's Table

Brett Younger

Some scholars suggest that every meal in literature is a communion scene. Could every meal in the Bible be a communion text? Could every passage be an invitation to God's grace? These meditations on the Lord's Supper help us listen to the myriad of ways God invites us to gratefully, reverently, and joyfully share the cup of Christ. 978-1-57312-720-2 246 pages/pb **$18.00**

A Time to Laugh
Humor in the Bible

Mark E. Biddle

With characteristic liveliness, Mark E. Biddle explores the ways humor was intentionally incorporated into Scripture. Drawing on Biddle's command of Hebrew language and cultural subtleties, A Time to Laugh guides the reader through the stories of six biblical characters who did rather unexpected things. 978-1-57312-683-0 164 pages/pb **$14.00**

A True Hope
Jedi Perils and the Way of Jesus

Joshua Hays

Star Wars offers an accessible starting point for considering substantive issues of faith, philosophy, and ethics. In A True Hope, Joshua Hays explores some of these challenging ideas through the sayings of the Jedi Masters, examining the ways the worldview of the Jedi is at odds with that of the Bible. 978-1-57312-770-7 186 pages/pb **$18.00**

To order call **1-800-747-3016** or visit **www.helwys.com**

Word of God Across the Ages
Using Christian History in Preaching
Bill J. Leonard

In this third, enlarged edition, Bill J. Leonard returns to the roots of the Christian story to find in the lives of our faithful forebears examples of the potent presence of the gospel. Through these stories, those who preach today will be challenged and inspired as they pursue the divine Word in human history through the ages. *978-1-57312-828-5 174 pages/pb* **$19.00**

The World Is Waiting for You
Celebrating the 50th Ordination Anniversary of Addie Davis
Pamela R. Durso & LeAnn Gunter Johns, eds.

Hope for the church and the world is alive and well in the words of these gifted women. Keen insight, delightful observations, profound courage, and a gift for communicating the good news are woven throughout these sermons. The Spirit so evident in Addie's calling clearly continues in her legacy. *978-1-57312-732-5 224 pages/pb* **$18.00**

William J. Reynolds
Church Musician
David W. Music

William J. Reynolds is renowned among Baptist musicians, music ministers, song leaders, and hymnody students. In eminently readable style, David W. Music's comprehensive biography describes Reynolds's family and educational background, his career as a minister of music, denominational leader, and seminary professor. *978-1-57312-690-8 358 pages/pb* **$23.00**

With Us in the Wilderness
Finding God's Story in Our Lives
Laura A. Barclay

What stories compose your spiritual biography? In *With Us in the Wilderness*, Laura Barclay shares her own stories of the intersection of the divine and the everyday, guiding readers toward identifying and embracing God's presence in their own narratives.
978-1-57312-721-9 120 pages/pb **$13.00**

To order call 1-800-747-3016 or visit www.helwys.com

Clarence Jordan's
Cotton Patch Gospel

The Complete Collection

Hardback • 448 pages
Retail 50.00 • Your Price 25.00

Paperback • 448 pages
Retail 40.00 • Your Price 20.00

The Cotton Patch Gospel, by Koinonia Farm founder Clarence Jordan, recasts the stories of Jesus and the letters of the New Testament into the language and culture of the mid-twentieth-century South. Born out of the civil rights struggle, these now-classic translations of much of the New Testament bring the far-away places of Scripture closer to home: Gainesville, Selma, Birmingham, Atlanta, Washington D.C.

More than a translation, *The Cotton Patch Gospel* continues to make clear the startling relevance of Scripture for today. Now for the first time collected in a single, hardcover volume, this edition comes complete with a new Introduction by President Jimmy Carter, a Foreword by Will D. Campbell, and an Afterword by Tony Campolo. Smyth & Helwys Publishing is proud to help reintroduce these seminal works of Clarence Jordan to a new generation of believers, in an edition that can be passed down to generations still to come.

SMYTH & HELWYS
To order call **1-800-747-3016**
or visit **www.helwys.com**

www.ingramcontent.com/pod-product-compliance
Lightning Source LLC
Chambersburg PA
CBHW070844160426
43192CB00012B/2299